Miracle
Faith

Miracle Faith

The Truth Revealed in the Mustard Seed

Wayne Weaver

Miracle Faith by Wayne Weaver
©2019 by Wayne Weaver

Most Scripture quotations are taken from the Holy Bible, King James Version (Public Domain).

One scripture quotation taken from The Holy Bible, New International Version® NIV® Copyright © 1973 1978 1984 2011 by Biblica, Inc. ™ Used by permission. All rights reserved worldwide.

Edited by Elaine Starner
Project Directed by Arlen Miller
Front Cover Photo of Murren, Switzerland by Wayne Weaver
Author Photo by Matthew Weaver

Printed in USA.
ISBN: 978-0-9910387-1-8 (Trade paperback)

Ministries of Wayne Weaver was established as a publishing arm of the ministry and call of God in the life of Pastor Wayne Weaver. Living in Ohio, Wayne has served as a 'tent-maker' minister for over thirty years. He has witnessed the hand of God through mighty moves of revival in the United States and in other countries. His calling is especially to help Christians who are struggling to overcome and to help the church realize the fullness of the plan of God.

For more information or additional books please contact us:

MINISTRIES OF
WAYNEWEAVER

531 Dover Rd. NE | Sugarcreek, Ohio 44681
www.MinistriesOfWayneWeaver.com

to my dear wife, Martha,

and our four children and their spouses,

Maurita and Jason,

Michael and Arie,

Monica and Dustin,

and Matthew and Rosetta,

and all their generations, until the return of Christ

Contents

Introduction

A few years ago, the Lord spoke deeply into my heart from the prophet Ezekiel and that began my quest for the deeper truth about faith.

> The diseased have ye not strengthened, neither have ye healed that which was sick, neither have ye bound up that which was broken, neither have ye brought again that which was driven away, neither have ye sought that which was lost; but with force and with cruelty have ye ruled them (Ezekiel 34:4).

Most of the above verse posed no problem for me. But the beginning is a rebuke about healing. "You haven't healed the sick," He was telling me.

I have found that most tend to draw back from walking under God's anointed healing hand. The cross that accompanies it is too great. I was no exception.

> [God] is able to do exceeding abundantly above all that we ask or think, according to the power that worketh in us (Ephesians 3:20).

According to this verse, I saw clearly that God is able in all things to do far beyond our thinking and asking, but His holy power has to work within us to bring the miracles.

God have mercy on me for my unbelief, and help me to be faithful in what You have shown me—Your answer to the deep cry within.

He has shown me the deeper truth of mustard seed faith, and this is why I wrote *Miracle Faith*.

I also realized that mustard seed faith is available for all. After we receive the revelation within, we can then also attain the kind of faith that prevails against mountains and produces miracles.

It's for everyone—everyone who believes.

Wayne Weaver

CHAPTER 1

Enemies of Faith

What is faith?
Why is faith important?
What is the purpose of faith?

The foundational truth of God's Word is faith. Faith is so important that without it we cannot please God.

It is an absolute requirement for all true children of God to walk in faith and by faith and through faith. There is no other God-given, overcoming power that man can have other than to overcome by faith.

Faith is the only way God can convey what He wants for us to become, be, and have. It is the heavenly avenue for God to administer His forgiveness, direction, blessings, mercy, and grace to fallen mankind.

Faith's purpose is to fulfill God's desire on earth as it is in heaven. It is to receive the promises of God from His hand, so that He alone is glorified. This faith is for salvation and principles of truth for actual workings within. Without the promises of God, we cannot even be saved.

✧

Now we see why the enemy stays busy against the children of God. Two specific enemies are at constant odds against spiritual faith in Almighty God, His promises, and His provisions for mankind. The two enemies are self, i.e., the carnal/natural man, and Lucifer—what a contrast!

I want to first identify the enemy of self. Self performs as a threefold entity—the natural man, the carnal man, and the self man, all functioning outside of faith. These three characters all work from the same root and produce the same product.

> Faith is an active embrace of the Word and promises of God on a daily basis

In ordinary, everyday duty or in their concept of spiritual duty, these three are all concerned about size (or self-image), formulas, and personal reward.

The self man has great misunderstanding of what the true spiritual life is all about and what he is to do concerning the will of God. He could get along well without faith in Christ— if it were not for the natural lost state of man. He needs Christ only when he needs forgiveness or gets into a difficult situation. The carnal man acknowledges he wants God's will, yet with conditions attached. But this is never God's way.

The carnal man often understands faith as a lifestyle. A devout lifestyle helps man to survive his own comfortable ways without seeking further for a deeper life in Christ. The carnal/natural/self man can do many nice things. He can duplicate things without dependence on Christ. Thus, we see the tares growing among the wheat.

True faith is not a lifestyle. The spiritual man is concerned about what kind of spiritual work is done, not what size it is. And finally, the spiritual man is concerned that God alone is glorified, regardless of what it costs.

> Every man's work shall be made manifest: for the day shall declare it, because it shall be revealed by fire; and the fire shall try every man's work of what sort it is (1 Corinthians 3:13).

Faith is an active embrace of the Word and promises of God on a daily basis, through the avenue of the cross of Christ. The spiritual man is constantly seeking to be led by the Spirit of God, and those so led are therefore called the sons of God.

We understand that the natural/carnal/self man cannot receive things from the Spirit of God and therefore does not see the importance or the purposes in the promises of Almighty God. This man does not understand what the promises of God are about. He lives under the law of the Word rather than under the spirit of the law.

> But the natural man receiveth not the things of the Spirit of God: for they are foolishness unto him: neither can he know them, because they are spiritually discerned (1 Corinthians 2:14).

The promises of God have been given to transform us from elements of darkness and personal depravity into the image and nature of Christ by the divine power of the Holy Spirit. The promises of God are not a luxury nor are they optional! Self demands evidence before believing, but the promises are to be received by faith alone, for God to be glorified! I strongly believe that faith is the only thing that brings eternal reward. Because that which is not of faith is sin!

Therefore all religious activity propagated by self will never be acceptable to God. The promises are not for flesh-produced good deeds and esteemed, self-made virility. Not for a minute! Only faith and works of faith (which I will cover later in the book) are the virtues that hold reward for God's glory.

Christ and the disciples, as well as Old Testament saints, walked by faith, and they subdued kingdoms, shut the mouths of lions, and raised the dead to life again. Since we do not wrestle against flesh and blood, what do we wrestle against? All our wrestling then is against spiritual things. This is not a concept; it is truth (unbiased reality), the way God sees all things from His perspective. Man's own power and strength cannot overcome anything that is spiritual. Man has to humble himself and confess his powerlessness and depravity before he will come to this wonderful truth that Jesus Himself declared.

> Then answered Jesus and said unto them, Verily, verily, I say unto you, The Son can do nothing of himself... (John 5:19).

Man without specific faith in the overcoming power of the provision and promises of God will never fight spiritual battles effectively. Instead, man will fight himself into tired and defeated misery or smile about his own achievements and say, "I am glad I am not like the publicans and sinners."

Publicans and sinners both sit at the same table in fellowship with genuine leanness toward God. They carry little burden and are quick to condemn and cast a critical eye. Their scope of magnification falls toward those who, with intensity and fervency, live godly in Christ Jesus.

Does all have to be done by faith alone? Yes, alone! Is faith then praying, asking, begging, sitting and waiting?

The disciples had just seen a man do miracles and were concerned that he was not a disciple. They forbade the man immediately.

> But Jesus said, Forbid him not: for there is no man which shall **do a miracle in my name, that can lightly speak evil of me** (Mark 9:39).

Why have the miracles ceased among so many who have professed Christ? Because the work that Christ is doing in our day is lightly spoken of as evil—in fact, mightily spoken against!

> For he that is not against us is on our part. For whosoever shall give you a cup of water to drink in my name, because ye belong to Christ, verily I say unto you, he shall not lose his reward. And whosoever shall offend one of these little ones that believe in me, it is better for him that a millstone were hanged about his neck, and he were cast into the sea (Mark 9:40-42).

It is only the little ones in the kingdom who will do true God-glorifying miracles.

> Verily I say unto you, Except ye be converted, and become as little children, ye shall not enter into the kingdom of heaven. Whosoever therefore shall humble himself as this little child, the same is greatest in the kingdom of heaven (Matthew 18:3-4).

The Bible is clear about what these people who live by faith and walk in faith are called. They are called kingdom people and are known as little children.

Many are much too proud and concerned about the opinion of the day to become as little children. This thinking is that of a "rich man," and the result of this spirit is that there are few who are able to enter the narrow gate.

The church of Laodicea became rich and increased with goods. How? By their own personal goals and masterful achievements they came to a place that God had not brought about. If their work and achievements would have been God's doing, He would have accepted it.

It is much easier for a carnal mind to muscle itself through life without faith in God's provision than it is to have faith in His promises. Self can be well able to produce Ishmael as Abram did. Ishmaels are easy to produce and require no faith.

Abram simply could not have children through Sarai because she was barren. Notice that Abram did not have a seed problem. He had a faith problem. He could not produce by faith. When there was a divine change in Abram's faith, God changed Abram's name to Abraham. I will give a full exposition on this divine change in chapter 7.

I also find that when God spoke to Abraham to take his son Isaac for an offering, God called Isaac Abraham's "only" son.

> And he said, **Take now thy son, thine only son Isaac**, whom thou lovest, and get thee into the land of Moriah; and offer him there for a burnt offering upon one of the mountains which I will tell thee of... And he said, Lay not thine hand upon the lad, neither do thou any thing unto him: for now I know that thou fearest God, seeing thou hast not **withheld thy son, thine only son** from me (Genesis 22:2, 12).

I have come to a place of accepting this truth of faith as non-optional, a spiritual requirement from God. This is the essential process even after you have received from God by faith.

> And said, By myself have I sworn, saith the LORD,
> for because thou hast done this thing, and hast not
> withheld thy son, thine only son: (Genesis 22:16).

We clearly understand that it was only the spiritual son of Abraham upon whom God could rest His spiritual blessing. Abraham had cried, saying, "Oh that Ishmael might live before God," and yet Abraham placed his Isaac (the son whom he had received by faith) upon the altar to die twenty-six years later!

Here is the big difference: Personal achievements seldom die, and if they do, it is a hard death. But spiritual promises that have been received by faith are always upon the altar before God. This blessing of Isaac became a metric for comparing nations of descendants to the stars of heaven and the sands of the seashore, because Isaac came by faith. But this was only after Abraham's willing knife rose above the tender, precious promise of what God miraculously performed after 99 years of proven impossibility.

> That in blessing I will bless thee, and in multiplying
> I will multiply thy seed as the stars of the heaven,
> and as the sand which is upon the sea shore; and
> thy seed shall possess the gate of his enemies
> (Genesis 22:17).

How do I know if I have given all as a spiritual sacrifice? The answer is clear: If you have found your life and not lost it first, you are probably a carnal man doing the things of God.

If you have lost your life for the sake of Christ, you will find it. The spiritual man lives under the power of the Holy Spirit and knows none else. Have you ever held the knife of sacrifice over the "It" in your life?

If you have lost your life before you have found it, you have truly lost it. Lost means lost! You will never find it in the condition you lost it in. You will lose the caterpillar and find the butterfly at the same place you laid all before the Lord in complete abandonment.

After someone has consecrated their life (lost their life), they will experience a distinct difference from their pre-consecration experience. If the person's thinking or inner heart condition is unchanged, frankly, the consecration didn't happen. That person has not lost their life.

It is through the losing of life that one finds their life. Finding means that person discovers a new life of meaning and effectiveness. A resurrection has occurred because a death (losing of life) has happened. And of course the only way a resurrection can happen is following a death (loss).

You lost the caterpillar and found the butterfly at the same place you laid all before the Lord in complete abandonment.

> He that findeth his life shall lose it: and he that loseth his life for my sake shall find it (Matthew 10:39).

I solemnly ask the question, *Have I truly found my life?* The true finding will be a transformed spiritual man. The transformed man will stay transformed by continual renewing of the mind, always proving what is the good, acceptable, and perfect will of God. Without being transformed, you will not know the will of God, because you will be serving your own will.

God's true children are all divinely transformed by the renewed mind. Now, the enemy will also try to duplicate this without the cross, but everything has to be born of God. The only way to overcome the world is by having all things born of God.

> For whatsoever is born of God overcometh the world: and this is the victory that overcometh the world, even our faith (1 John 5:4).

What is a *whatsoever*? Whatsoever is everything! Everything has to be born of God by faith to overcome. Whatsoevers have to be laid at the foot of the cross in order for them to be resurrected in the power of Almighty God. If it is not born of God, it is of the world, regardless what it looks like. Someone may believe that wearing a certain article of clothing in a certain way is overcoming the world. The Bible is clear that overcoming the world is not in wearing or not wearing.

The question we need to ask ourselves is: Are my achievements recognized in eternity, regardless of how good they might look to man's eyes?

The other enemy of faith is Lucifer and his powers. He will try to create confusion concerning the power of faith, calling it mythical, dangerous, or strange. He will transform himself as an angle of light, working through humans with many forms, formulas, impressions, and imitations of the truth of the Bible. He has used people to act in such a manner to deter the underpowered so that they remain powerless.

But what will be obvious is that all his actions will not exhibit life. People may experience something that seems miraculous to human eyes, but it will carry no power to bring forth spiritual, heavenly life over a tested time period.

Jannes and Jambres were the magicians when Moses was standing before Pharaoh, seeking Israel's exodus from Egypt.

> Now as Jannes and Jambres withstood Moses, so do these also resist the truth: men of corrupt minds, reprobate concerning the faith (2 Timothy 3:8).

These corrupt men did almost every miracle that God did through Moses—but with one decisive and notable exception. They could not bring even the tiniest bit of life out of dust. These Egyptian magicians confessed that only the finger of God could turn dust to lice (see Exodus 8:19).

This is an interesting observation and confession by these corrupt, occultist men. God Almighty holds the only authority as Creator and Life-giver in all the universe! The life-giving power is within His dominion and spiritual authority alone.

God's holiness can never be duplicated, implied, or imitated. His claim to holiness is eternal and remains forever supernal. Lucifer can never change or duplicate the character of true life flowing from the glorious presence of Almighty God. Almighty God is eternal life! Lucifer is eternal death!

The characteristics of these two kingdoms will never mix nor are they ever difficult to distinguish. This distinction between the two kingdoms can be discerned spiritually if you will look at one basic ingredient of God's true character. It is holiness. Without it, no man can see God.

I am amazed at the cost of the great work of the baptism of the Holy Spirit.

The latter day—that now has become evident—will bring an influx of lawlessness and evil so deceptive that God will take the elect home early, or else they will be deceived by apparent forms of luciferic equivalence. Transformed angels of light!

The ambush by deception starts within the fallen church. Fallen from where? Fallen from the power of the Holy Spirit as the empowerment that fills all in all! Fallen from the life and true faith in the assembly of the people of God.

This fall starts with the people of God seeking answers outside the truth of God. The end time will open the pits of luciferic assertions influencing personality disorders with obvious imprints of demonic activity. The church will refuse to deal with this activity as a spiritual problem, and this will leave the church in limbo. This will be the beginning of the division of sheep and goats. If the ways of Egypt fill counseling centers with every form of carnal analysis instead of dealing with deep spiritual roots that are often overlooked and considered irrelevant, the apostasy of the church will linger in powerlessness. When victims are only taught how *to cope* with sin and its issues, they will remain bound by curses and devils. This approach to help the sad soul is no different than what the world system has to offer. In fact, the church has learned from the world. Bible seminaries are plagued by humanist professors and educators who know little about the power of God and the Holy Spirit. What a sad picture in this last day.

Jesus and His disciples never had a center to counsel the stricken. They laid hands on people and cast out devils, and every last person was set free. The contemporary church of this age has lost the power of the Holy Spirit and turned to the world of Egypt for help.

> Woe to them that go down to Egypt for help; and stay on horses, and trust in chariots, because they are many; and in horsemen, because they are very strong; but they look not unto the Holy One of Israel, neither seek the LORD! Now the Egyptians are men, and not God; and their horses flesh, and not spirit. When the LORD shall stretch out his hand, both he that helpeth shall fall, and he that is holpen shall fall down, and they all shall fail together (Isaiah 31:1, 3).

This is precisely the place where many traditional and worldly churches have arrived. We now trust in man, and warn against the Holy Spirit. The authentic power of God will always be uncomfortable for the sinners.

There is a tendency within man's reasoning to perceive the power of the Holy Spirit as dangerous. However, I understand with scriptural clarity the eternal danger of questioning the miraculous power of God to free a soul from strongholds. That is the hour when Lucifer will open the flood gates of deception, with miracles and signs and wonders and having meetings in dry places, saying, "Here is the kingdom and there is the kingdom," when the kingdom is within.

> And he said unto the disciples, The days will come, when ye shall desire to see one of the days of the Son of man, and ye shall not see it (Luke 17:22).

That day is our day! Oh, to see the power of the Holy Spirit working like it was in the days of Jesus!

I have lived the Spirit-filled life for nearly forty years, and this is the cry I have heard for all those years. There is a secret longing in those hungry for God to restore His power in the church.

But the pulpits are saying it is not for our day, and they call any move of faith "outdated" and "deceptive."

This stops the power and work of the Holy Spirit in the church—and causes many to sit at ease and be comfortable. They adopt a system of rules and guidelines of practice without true faith. Within one generation, the transcendent glory of God quickly becomes unknown.

I have also noticed another reaction, often formed as a rebellion to the system of rules and guidelines. This begins with good intentions and an experience in the power of God, but then the door is opened for miracles by man—but without a life of holiness. This is not from God. God's demonstrations of power always also display His holy nature. .

Some poor, sin-laden souls will turn toward these leaders and experience miracles; and because their hearts know little about the nature of God and His holiness, after some years they will turn toward lusts and sexual slavery and follow these to a place of despair.

Here we see two ditches along the sides of the road, and both are driven by self. Both of these reactions stem back to a resistance to the real and authentic power of God.

We can all find examples of humans who have been transformed through mystical and occult overtones claimed to be of faith but which turn many into paths of deception. Can it be understood any other way than that the enemy wants to see Almighty God displeased with the generation of redeemed mankind?

The church has lost its power of the Holy Spirit, therefore it will lose its power to transform those in heavy bondages and sin.

When a church has lost the power of transformation, it has lost the power to conform to the image of Christ as well. A true transformation is needed before we can be conformed to the image of Christ. This is all and alone by faith.

Conforming to the image of Christ is not accomplished by a set of rules but by transformation through faith in Almighty God. It is in these scenarios that there are often luciferic footprints of deception in some form at work in manifested miracles.

Where else would the enemy choose to place his footprint, attempting to deter the weakened and blinded church to fear the power of God? The enemy will try to duplicate the power of God in every way possible—but there will be one powerful missing element: the very nature of the life of God, which is His holiness. And His Holiness can never be copied. If you see demonstrators of mighty power without the cross or the holiness of God, know one thing assuredly: Those demonstrations are not from Almighty God but are a wicked counterfeit to frighten the ineffective church so that it remains powerless.

There are many who try to duplicate the laying on of hands and praying for the sick. And many such things are done as an attempt to prove power and to intrigue wondering minds. But unless there is an attraction to the life of the cross and God's imputed holiness as foundational truth within, these are only imitations of the real. When miracles and signs and wonders are a greater attraction than the cross of Christ, then Christ is not the author of those works.

You can also know these demonstrations are not genuine but pretense when the cross of Christ is professed but there are no signs that follow. Because...

"These signs shall follow them that believe; In my name shall they cast out devils; they shall speak with new tongues;" (Mark 16:17).

I experienced the power of the baptism of the Holy Spirit many years ago. I had never been taught about what I experienced that solemn day in the presence of God. I had never heard the phrase *baptism of the Holy Spirit.* I found it alone, weeping in my closet and seeking God for something I was missing—yet not knowing what it was. My life was helplessly powerless and heavy laden with sin, yet well accepted in the church. But after the baptism of the Holy Spirit, I was immediately rejected by the nominal church I was part of, and I became a stranger to the acceptance of man.

I indeed baptize you with water unto repentance: but he that cometh after me is mightier than I, whose shoes I am not worthy to bear: he shall baptize you with the Holy Ghost, and with fire: Whose fan is in his hand, and he will thoroughly purge his floor, and gather his wheat into the garner; but he will burn up the chaff with unquenchable fire (Matthew 3:11-12).

The fire of cleansing has been so severe at times that without the presence of Christ, I would never have survived.

Personal confrontations that can be expected from the world are like dust on a scale compared to the viciousness that can come from carnal Christians not walking in the Spirit.

Oh, the hurt and pain as the mentality of carnal men passes judgment against spiritual men, judgment based upon their own interpretation of the Word of God. The depth of this fire goes deeper than any natural fire could ever burn. It reveals any form of self that could still be alive in hidden places in the heart.

The carnal repression is severe and relentless from the man of Cain, Esau, Saul, and the harlot. If you walk as sons of God in this day of religious corruption, the enemy is relentless. The accusation against a spiritual man may seem accurate and astute to the carnal imagination. Yet the foundation of the carnal man is a snake pit of venom designed to destroy the true saints of God. It causes all carnal men to fear the very presence of God's men and count them as dung and useless.

If we do not have spiritual eyes, giving in to carnal self-defense when under such attack will solidly destroy us. My life always needs to respond to God in a broken and humble spirit. My understanding is that my personal life needs much deeper cleansing than what I can behold in the light of my own mirror. The chastening of the Lord is necessary for the Holy Spirit to be the Comforter within His temple.

I am amazed at the cost of the great work of the baptism of the Holy Spirit. The greater the anointing, the greater the cross!

From the strength of the cross bursts forth a powerful anointing. I thank God Almighty for the power of the cross. It keeps the spiritual man broken and humble, and herein lies the power of the Holy Spirit. God uses the fire for His glory, to bring the wheat into His storehouse.

It was through the first several years of my walk in the Holy Spirit that I was welcomed to mainline charismatic-type movements because I was deeply rejected everywhere else. After several years of fellowship, God turned my heart away from what I saw.

I was led to go the way of the cross and live a life embracing the depth of God's transformation through death and resurrection. God led me to partake of His divine nature in true holiness, with power and demonstration of the Holy Spirit. In this wilderness of loneliness is where I became a personal friend to true men of God.

I consider my life a precious offering to the One who suffered for this wonderful freedom I know.

What happened to our generation? The lukewarm seemingly are the only ones who do not feel out of place in church meetings. In a lukewarm environment, offering money is needed more than holiness and the power of Almighty God. The church sports team takes time to pray that the other church team would be defeated so that God can be glorified. I have observed among some churches that the sports practice sessions are the main concern of church goals of the year. These are real conditions of popular churches.

Lucifer has done much to hide the true people of God by bringing much activity to create captivity. How else can the enemy convene in the last evil days except through lukewarm, out-of-touch Christianity?

Let us be completely aware that the two different kingdoms will be operating at the same time, both in the supernatural, but with distinct differences. The counterfeit will operate in the supernatural with *self* as the forefront, in worldly tenor promoting lawlessness as freedom to do anything. The true will operate in the supernatural with spiritual *holiness*, denying self at the cross for freedom from the evil without. One calls lawlessness freedom, and the other will experience freedom from lawlessness.

The real mark of true saints is a clear display of internal holiness from God. The other visible mark is life.

> He that hath the Son hath life; and he that hath not the Son of God hath not life (1 John 5:12).

If we do not have life, we do not have Jesus, regardless of what was experienced.

The only thing positive about the dire conditions I have described is this: This is where God has placed His faithful ones. These are the days of Elijah. These are prime conditions to have faith in a God who will not forsake the righteous. These are prime conditions for God to shake both the lukewarm and cold-hearted sinners. Elijah will come again with a latter rain that the world has never seen before. It will be more glorious than the earlier rain. It will come when men of God have faith in the promises of God once again.

> Be patient therefore, brethren, unto the coming of the Lord. Behold, the husbandman waiteth for the precious fruit of the earth, and hath long patience for it, until he receive the **early** and **latter** rain (James 5:7).

In these conditions, we find the real ones who carry the holiness and power of God. They are the weeping saints, casting their burdens before the throne of Almighty God through personal intercession. They are crying for true revival once again, asking that the power of the Holy Spirit and holiness would come back into the home, the church, and the local community.

This is not the time to lose faith in the power of God. The prayer closets are starting to fill up again. Yes, there are men and women leaving their beds early in the morning and seeking the face of God. It is happening around the world. Will you be one of these dear ones?

CHAPTER 2

Conditions of Faith

What am I to do as a believer concerning faith?

The answer is clear! I am called primarily to please God, so that He is glorified as I am transformed into the image of Christ and walk in God's will.

God wants heaven's demonstration of power to achieve His purpose on earth. Throughout this book, I will seek to bring understanding of God's call for us.

The invisible forces of the power of darkness will try hard to throw dark and stormy clouds over the minds of the true spiritual believer. Lucifer and his forces will certainly try to cast difficult shadows around God's children so that they will tend to believe only what is visible. I understand that it takes no faith at all to believe what is seen. These powers of darkness aim to inflict deep discouragement and a helpless feeling upon the children of God.

The spiritual man will quickly run to the precious provision in the cross and pour out his heaviness and despair onto that life-cleansing tree. He will there find the power of a broken life. He will find his comfort zone of faith in the balance of Biblical wisdom and truth.

Before I can go deeper with Christ, I have two huge obstacles that must be overcome. Clearly, there is only one way to overcome these obstacles—it is by our faith.

For the believer to have the power of God within:

1. Self must die for the spiritual man to resurrect by the power of the Holy Spirit.

2. The love of the world must be overcome.

Depleted of self

One of the primary conditions where faith operates is when man is depleted from his own power, ability, and strength. God designed the truth of faith as an acceptable means to walk in His power in our earthen vessels. The self/natural man can never walk in this power.

There is no provision for a holy God to accept my carnal man. My carnal man must die without reservation. Self will always be the enemy of God's purpose, the biggest obstacle that stands in the way of pleasing God.

Self is so great an enemy to God that it is impossible for man ruled by self to receive the things from the Spirit of God. Self is never subject to the law of God, neither can it be. Self is concerned about equality and self-esteem, so that it is well thought of by its contemporaries. Self is motivated to portray its self-esteeming opinions upon fellows of higher importance. When a superior thinks well of a self-motivated person, he does well. When his peers devalue him, he is ready to fight to impress, even if he has to cast someone to the dust.

Jesus was a spiritual man and pursued no reputation. Yet He saw that he was fashioned among the best. When Jesus saw who He really was, He saw the prime opportunity of faith. He chose the path of the spiritual man and humbled Himself, so that He could die the death of the cross. In faith, He stooped face-down to earth, in servanthood and true obedience, and died to human nature and all its suggestions. This was the cross death.

The cross death is now the spiritual experience that bears a promise like none other. It is only this cross death that promises the fundamental change of resurrection from its own death.

> But made himself of no reputation, and took upon him the form of a servant, and was made in the likeness of men: And being found in fashion as a man, he humbled himself, and became obedient unto death, even the death of the cross (Philippians 2:7-8).

The self within man must surrender and die. This is a condition for faith to find a new beginning. In this spiritual death, we become entirely vulnerable and completely dependent on heaven's supreme power to resurrect us in newness of life.

As long as the natural man sees hope in himself, he will not surrender at the final place of death—the cross of Christ.

When Abram saw this, he surrendered. I must bring Abram back into this picture again. He was well able to have children. We see this when he produced Ishmael. What Abram could not do was have children by faith. Sarai was barren. I recognize that my Sarai is also barren, but my Hagar is not. It is easy to produce with Hagar, because I can do it without faith. But the *promise* is in the son of Sarai.

Who is your Hagar and who is your Sarai? Hagar is from Sinai in Arabia. Another way to bring understanding to this is that Hagar is in the forty-year wilderness of unbelief in the Sinai desert, where human power and the will of self prevail. However, the only place where I can produce by the power of Almighty God is in Canaan, the land filled by the promises of God. This is not the self-empowered desert of unbelief. This is a higher place, called Jerusalem, the birth womb of us all, and here alone is where God is glorified because He is the one who accomplishes what is done through faith.

I must embrace the following verses.

> For this Agar is mount Sinai in Arabia, and answereth to Jerusalem which now is, and is in bondage with her children. But Jerusalem which is above is free, which is the mother of us all. For it is written, Rejoice, thou barren that bearest not; break forth and cry, thou that travailest not: for the desolate hath many more children than she which hath an husband. Now we, brethren, as Isaac was, are the children of promise. But as then he that was born after the flesh persecuted him that was born after the Spirit, even so it is now (Galatians 4:25-29).

It is the deception of my self man that delights in noteworthy personal achievements for God. According to these verses, God does not see things this way at all.

For example, with all the great things that Jacob did in the eyes of man, there were only two reasons that God placed him in the hall of faith (Hebrews chapter 11). Jacob had done good things, but among the things that he did were many that were not good—even in the eyes of man. Only after his surrender at Jabbok did God walk with him. Before this heavenly event, God watched Jacob with His eyes. After Jabbok, God led Jacob by His hand.

This is what Jacob did to merit God's commendation of faith: Jacob blessed Joseph's two sons from a marriage with an Egyptian woman, which was a direct violation of Jewish law, and Jacob worshipped, leaning on a stick! The self man hates leaning. He can do so much better walking on his own. At least, that's what he thinks.

What does God think? When God sees me walking alone, He sees me walking independently of Him. He sees that I will not need faith to accomplish anything. He does not count me as righteous, but as self-righteous.

Can I at once acknowledge the fact that God cannot accept anything that is not of faith?

> For whatsoever is not of faith is sin (Romans 14:23).

Am I declaring that if I walk leaning on my own effort to produce good will, that is called unbelief? Most certainly! It is actually called sin, because it is done without faith. If I can do it without faith, I declare I can do it without God.

Certainly I can, without much problem, do many nice works that are not of faith. But what is produced without faith is my self-made Ishmael.

When Abraham came face-to-face with this truth, he cried:

> And Abraham said unto God, O that Ishmael might live before thee! (Genesis 17:18)

What he was really saying was, "Oh, that God could accept my own works in my attempt to produce the promise."

As we have noted before, we acknowledge that Abram could reproduce—because he produced an Ishmael. What Abram could not do was produce a child by faith.

Here I see the condition of faith: moving away from our ability and moving to believing by faith in His ability. When we have faith, God's hand upon us is released to produce what we cannot produce ourselves. And this is the key to receiving the promises of God.

This is the key to the source of overcoming power.

This is important to understand lest we become hopeless and unfruitful in our lives of faith.

> For it is written, Rejoice, thou barren that bearest not; break forth and cry, thou that travailest not: for the desolate hath many more children than she which hath an husband (Galatians 4:27).

You can produce a thousand things by yourself, or two things by faith. Self man will gloat over a thousand things. But God says that the two things produced by faith makes the man far richer, because moth and rust cannot corrupt that wealth, and those who live by faith will stand in the presence of God as children who were produced by His power alone.

God sees "Isaacs" who are the result of faith. They might not look like much in man's opinion, but God doesn't judge like man does. He takes note of all things produced by faith through a fully surrendered soul. God does not consider what is done by our own effort. God looks at the source, not the size.

So shall I discontinue doing all things that are not done by faith? That which is not of faith is sin.

Victory by Christ's power alone

The life that I now live is by the power of the Holy Spirit alone. Herein lies the condition of faith in all matters visible and invisible alike. Herein is the overcoming of the second obstacle that prevents me from going deeper with Christ— the love of the world.

> **Love not the world**, neither the **things that are in** the world. If any man love the world, the love of the Father is not in him (1 John 2:15).

I must have a clear picture what the world is, in order to understand what I need to overcome. If *world* is anything exterior, it is easy and quick to deal with and I will not need faith to overcome it. The meaning of the word *world* is in the form of three specific enemies of ours: two kinds of lust and personal pride. It is the longings of the eyes, longings of my natural self life, and pride of *bios*, (i.e., what I can produce). In Greek, it is this: (al-ad-zon-i'-a) braggadocio, i.e. (by implication) self-possession. My pedigree. My bio.

I have no better way to explain what *world* is than to call it leaven. It is like a poisonous infection of the eye and the inner man. It is puffy and intent on making "little me" look very big, to compete and outdo by the strength of my own infected confidence. *World* within will keep me from faith, and it will keep me from receiving by faith. *World* is, in part, *man's own effort.*

One of the hardest things to overcome is this world within. A million years of my own effort to overcome *that* world will never touch the surface of deliverance from it, regardless of who I am. Yet, many consider themselves quite successful at it.

> The whole secret to the life of faith points to being crucified with Christ.

There is only one way to overcome this poisonous leaven, according to the Bible. If I think I have achieved overcoming the world in any other way, then I must confess that I do not know what Jesus calls "world."

Many are blind to the fact it is by faith alone that we overcome this world.

> For **whatsoever is born of God** overcometh the world: and this is the victory that overcometh the world, even **our faith** (1 John 5:4).

Faith that overcomes the world and impossible situations is not a lifestyle—an idea we would want to comfort ourselves with. I find it popular among so many professing Christians to interpret faith as a lifestyle or set of Bible-based ideas. Faith is not a groove or a set standard of ideas toward God. Faith is the substance of things hoped for and the evidence of things not seen.

> Now faith is the substance of things hoped for, the evidence of things not seen. For by it the elders obtained a good report (Hebrews 11:1-2).

Again, there is nothing in this verse to give us any indication that faith is a culture, lifestyle, or set of ideas followed by repetition.

My confidence has to be with God and the power of God to do all things. Does this mean I cannot do anything independently of God? I answer yes. Indeed, it is possible to do things without acknowledging God. However, the Word still makes it clear that anything done without faith is of sin. This is how I understand this passage, and it has become my experience. This will also confound the carnal/natural man with unrealistic questions, such as, "Can I not clean windows without faith or mow my yard without faith?" The answer is simple—what is not of faith is sin.

> And he that doubteth is damned if he eat, because he eateth not of faith: for whatsoever is not of faith is sin (Romans 14:23).

The word *faith* is found only twice in the Old Testament but 247 times in the New Covenant (New Testament). A life of faith may be described as inviting God into the moment of everything we do, say, and are. All my going and doing I live by the faith of the Son of God because of who I am in Christ.

There are three kinds of "faith" recorded in the New Testament.

1. *Elpis* (1680 S.C.) means to anticipate, usually with pleasure.

2. *Oligopistos* (3640 S.C.) means incredulous, i.e., lacking of confidence in Christ.

3. *Pistis* (4102 S.C.) means persuasion of truth.

The Word is clear that our faith overcomes the world. There are no cultural lifestyles that overcome the world in a spiritual way. I can fight the lusts within with a clenched fist and win by the power of my own strong self man. There is only one problem—my self man is still me, and I overcame me! How can I overcome me? There has to be a power higher than I that can overcome that which I am.

There is only one man like myself who experienced this from the beginning of the New Covenant. The man Christ Jesus was in the form of me and died both a real and a spiritual death by the cross. How can I say it was a spiritual death? Because He could have called twelve legions of angels and escaped the cross. Instead, He died to all His ability, whether spiritual or natural. It all died at Calvary,

> I am crucified with Christ: nevertheless I live; yet not I, but Christ liveth in me: and **the life which I now live in the flesh I live by the faith of the Son of God**, who loved me, and gave himself for me (Galatians 2:20).

The whole secret to the life of faith points to being crucified with Christ.

Paul did not say "I try to" or "I want to be" crucified with Christ. He said "I *am* crucified with Christ." Until this statement becomes my true confession by experience, I will not understand the rest of the verse.

And because all of Christ's ability died at Calvary, it was all brought back to life again by another power higher than the death that cleaved His body. The Holy Spirit was the greater power. Jesus, the only begotten Son of God, was resurrected by the working of the Holy Spirit. This is exactly how the operation works!

> But **if the Spirit** of him that raised up Jesus from the dead dwell in you, he that raised up Christ from the dead shall also quicken your mortal bodies by his Spirit that dwelleth in you (Romans 8:11).

When I am crucified with Christ, I am dead. However, my heart is still active and so are my hands. But the life that lives in my earthen vessel is not me or the self man anymore. This life which I now live is by the faith of Jesus.

This is how we overcome the world: by our faith in the death and resurrection of Christ! The battle is between faith and the "world," defined as my natural performance sustained by my own stubborn nature.

We have all tried to curb ourselves with personal rules and extreme discipline, and we look back on our proud accomplishments and then fall flat on our face again. Jesus has made one provision so that I can become a true overcomer. I overcome by my faith through Christ and never by a lifestyle of a personal set of laws. I repeat, if I think I can achieve this overcoming power by any other means than what Jesus said, then I must conclude I do not understand *world* or *faith*.

There are only two ways that Christ has made available for me to overcome. I have to refer back to what I have written before. The Holy Bible does not say whosoever, but *whatsoever* is born of God overcomes the world. Nothing can be spiritually born without a death.

I understand that I can say that I am born-again and yet find many things in my life that have never died. This is why the Word says *whatsoever* is born of God overcomes the world.

God has to deal with my deep inner self and secrets that do not want to be brought to light so that I can honestly come to grips with who I am. This alone brings me to an acceptable humility, regardless of what I might appear to be.

All the deep facets of my own personal life have to be opened in the presence of God by His holy fire alone. Until the deep whatsoevers have died and are then born of God, His glory will not burn within my soul in purity and truth.

Hidden shadows of death can only be expelled by the power of the light of the risen Savior. Truth and light have to visit the deepest secrets of my soul before my whatsoevers become born of God. The rooms of sin, corruption, and ill-will within the treasure trove of my darkened past will have to die by exposure to the lamp of God's marvelous light. Until then, the world within will not rest nor will it die, but it simmers as smoldering ash under the silent terrors of guilt and personal touchiness.

When there has been no death and resurrection within, my understanding of God and His Word is distorted and the voice of His Spirit is silenced. My eyes stay blind, my tongue stays inflamed, my ears misinterpret, my hands remain powerless, and my feet find their own path away from the serenity of God. If this inner condition remains, my life will see things incorrectly and understand things incorrectly. My own will speaks things incorrectly and interprets things incorrectly. In this deprived condition, I wonder why I do not have a better understanding of faith that works the mighty work of Almighty God.

The solution is an earth-bending experience in deep, deep penitence before God. A deep cry of truth from heaven and a responding cry from within, confessing, "God, I am exactly what You see in me! I bring before You all my sin and my sins, and acknowledge my iniquity before You. I will no more live pretending what I should be. I will live in honesty and in truth and embrace Your holy nature within me. I no longer belong to myself, but I am now Your child and delight to be led by Your Holy Spirit. Baptize me now with Your baptism of the Holy Spirit. Amen!"

Oh, I acknowledge that if a drunkard spends his day next to a full bottle of whiskey, his temptation will be stronger than if he stays far away from that bottle. But the problem is not the bottle; it is the desire within the members of his body that are bound by the addiction to the bottle. Until the addiction has been broken by the power of God, this man will struggle until he dies or self dies. You see, sin lives in the members of the carnal/flesh/natural man.

> For when we were in the flesh, the motions of sins, which were by the law, did work in our members to bring forth fruit unto death (Romans 7:5).

What is this verse saying? If we are in the flesh, sin comes out of us because we are under law. Where there is no law, there is no violation.

> For until the law sin was in the world: but sin is not imputed when there is no law (Romans 5:13).

The only way to remove violation from the law is to remove law. So how do I remove law? I can never remove law, because it was given by a higher authority than I.

The only possible way to overcome this law is if God, Jesus, or the Holy Spirit would remove it so that we are no longer under it. If we could be brought above the law, we could prevail. Law brings death, but Christ is above the law of sin and death, and when we are in Christ, then we are also above the law of sin and death. I conclude then that it was done and it is finished through the death and resurrection of Christ!

> For the law of the Spirit of life in Christ Jesus hath made me free from the law of sin and death (Romans 8:2).

The truth of this revelation is the key of all keys in the life of faith. The phrase *in Christ* is found 77 times in the New Testament. That phrase is completely life changing! So the sin and death law was replaced by another law. It is the law of the Spirit of life *in Christ Jesus* that gives me freedom over the sin I so deeply hate.

With my mind I serve the law of the Spirit of life *in Christ Jesus,* but if I walk in the flesh, I will serve the other law that will cause me to sin.

> I thank God through Jesus Christ our Lord. So then with the mind I myself serve the law of God; but with the flesh the law of sin (Romans 7:25).

Daily I have these two options before me. One is the law of *do nots* and the other is the law of *dos.* The one that I focus on is the one I walk in. If my focus is on *do not,* I am certain to fall into the very thing that I do not wish to do. This is exactly what Paul was saying.

> For that which I do I allow not: for what I would, that do I not; but what I hate, that do I (Romans 7:15).

Let's ask ourselves an honest and personal question. Am I guided by dos, or am I guided by do nots?

Will I take up the cross and die to self and live in the Spirit? Or will I walk in the flesh and have the law of condemnation hanging over my head as I try harder to refrain from doing that which God is not pleased with? It is a daily choice.

If you choose the law over the unregenerated nature, you will have sinful results, and that is not of faith. If you choose the law of the Spirit, He will enable you to overcome, and Christ becomes the Victor! Herein is the condition of faith.

Here God comes to the rescue with tremendous power from heaven and gives man the power to bring healings and cast mountains into the sea. This is a hard thing for the flesh to accept, because it loves to receive trophies unto itself.

Here God is pleased, because God alone receives the praise of being your enabling and overcoming power. This is the condition God is seeking to display His miracle-working power in the impossibilities we face. He wants to see us victorious over the besetting sin in our lives. He wants to see us crush strongholds that have the magnitude of biblical Jericho!

Faith in God's Word

God's adopted and acceptable design for mankind is to walk in obedience to the truth by faith. This condition is where God becomes pleased with redeemed mankind.

We see that the conditions of faith start deep in the heart of a man who will not argue with God's Word, but only believe God's Word. He will never seek to change God's Word, but will be changed by God's Word.

When Abram started his journey from Haran after his father died, he saw and knew nothing except what God had spoken to him. God had told him to take a step out of where he was.

> Now the Lord had said unto Abram, Get thee out of thy country, and from thy kindred, and from thy father's house, unto a land that I will shew thee. (Genesis 12:1)

God didn't show Abram the land and say "Go there." God said, "Leave, and then I will show you the land."

I have experienced this same truth in different times of my life. Yet I wanted to know all that was before me. I turned to my reasoning powers and filled in the blanks. To my humiliation and dismay, I failed the path of faith. I have found that I must instead wait patiently until God directs my path.

God is seeking to display His miracle-working power in the impossibilities we face.

Waiting is spiritual. And patience is indeed a virtue. It grows as a fruit of the Spirit, and it is not grown in a hurry.

When God directs, there are no blanks that need to be filled in. We only walk by faith—which means we will not walk by sight.

The reason many have not seen the land of faith is because they have never left the country of unbelief. This can only be done in faith by hearing by the Word. This would be an extremely unpopular move in our day. Most professing Christians would not tolerate such a life of faith.

Biblical heroes, including Abram, Joseph, Moses, Paul, and many others were commanded by God to "come out of." This pattern is obvious among God's men of faith. When God leads us into a life of faith, He gives us small specifics and observes our obedience, measuring how far we can be led into His future of heavenly ambassadorship. Faith operates where God's spiritual children experience situations that cannot be changed by human hand. It operates as substance in something hoped for where evidence is not seen by human sight.

Faith that is seen is not faith. Impossibilities are the perfect situation where faith can operate with little resistance from the spiritual man. I have seen impossible things change right before my eyes. In the calling God has placed upon my life, I have witnessed many true miracles in the last forty years, including curses removed from people and healing of chronic problems of sick people who had no hope of recovery. A week seldom passes that I do not witness a miracle that most would not want to believe. Many would easily be offended at this, because there seems to be a submission to religious dignity and pride from the soul that naturally denies the miraculous power of God in this way.

To deny that there is absolute power to heal sickness in our day is the sin of unbelief. Many church-attending unbelievers become offended when God does a clear work of His mighty power. It was the same in the days of Jesus. Cain still gets envious and will always try to misunderstand and misinterpret the heart and worship of Abel. He will try to bring death to God's heavenly en-Abel-ed children.

There have been instances when the Lord gave me faith to believe in His name for healing, and healing is always received. I have seen many mighty works happen for God's glory! However, I seldom talk about this.

The question arises at times: Is the healing according to my faith or someone else's faith? The answer is found in Matthew 9:29.

> Then touched he their eyes, saying, According to your faith be it unto you.

Some have argued that if some do not receive healing and it brings them under condemnation, wouldn't it therefore be better to have unbelief?

Condemnation is not based on being healed or not being healed. Condemnation is a result of not being in Christ Jesus and therefore walking in the flesh.

> There is therefore now **no condemnation to them which are in Christ Jesus**, who walk not after the flesh, but after the Spirit (Romans 8:1).

If you listen to the excuses when a sick person is not healed, it becomes clear why healing is often not received. One of those excuses is that "God can receive more glory through my sickness than if I am healed." Then the personal choice has become sickness.

When a person says these words or something similar, I know immediately that it is not an expression of faith but evidence of unbelief. Such a person does not understand the promises in God's Word, and they are not ready to receive healing. A majority of people do not know God's will concerning healing and, as a result, question if it is God's will.

This comes from not understanding the promises of Almighty God.

When Jesus healed, was it not to bring glory to God? Has unbelief changed this glory? How many times have you glorified and thanked God when you heard someone had an incurable disease or a sickness leading to death? How many times have you glorified God when someone was healed?

There have been things in my own life that have been healed in a miraculous way and other things that have not been healed. Do I understand this? My answer is no. But I am not condemned by it at all.

Just last week the doctor told me a fast, powerful bacterial staph infection had eaten away my left eardrum, with no trace of it left. My hearing disappeared, and the doctor said it would never come back, unless there was a miracle. In all of his forty-plus years as a specialist and licensed M.D., he has never witnessed anything like it.

Will God want to restore my hearing? I do not yet know. I will wait on His answer to me so that I can pray effectively in the will of God.

I have come back to this area of writing after two weeks to say that the doctor saw a miracle he has never seen before. My eardrum is now completely healed. According to tests performed in a sound room, my hearing is perfect.

If it was the doctor who healed me, then thanks be to the doctor, but he had said he could not do anything about the eardrum. He was bewildered.

It was not the doctor. It was the power of Jesus that healed me after a man prayed over me. So who gets the glory? The Healer from Galilee!

We have to understand that the Israel that left Egypt could not enter the Promised Land because of unbelief. There were only two people of that generation who entered—Joshua and Caleb. It was not Israel's sin of idolatry, fornication, and moral issues that kept them from entering the Promised Land. It was their sin of unbelief.

> So we see that they could not enter in because of unbelief (Hebrews 3:19).

Some would argue that the sins I mentioned (idolatry, fornication, and moral issues) are unbelief. I appeal that these come as a result of unbelief. This foundational rebellion against God finds expression when His Word becomes optional.

It is clear that God was teaching Israel to have faith in His Word. He humbled them and took away their sustenance so they could receive food by faith alone. I have seen the desert they walked in. It is lifeless. Grass cannot grow. Trees are almost impossible to find. It was impossible for them to grow any food. Oh, yes, they knew how to bake bread and could do it very well back in Egypt! But God led them into a place where there was no grain. The bakers and the hunters and the farmers were out of commission.

God led them into this forty-year extreme desert to teach them something about their future. They needed to learn to conquer the unknown before them by the power of God's spoken Word! God's children needed to learn to have faith in the entire spoken Word while they were still in the dry deserts of Sinai so that they could live by the promises of God. They needed faith to overcome the seven cities of Canaan. We have the same seven cities to overcome by faith before the promises will be received by faith.

> And he humbled thee, and suffered thee to hunger, and fed thee with manna, which thou knewest not, neither did thy fathers know; that he might make thee know that man doth **not live by bread only**, but by **every word that proceedeth out of the mouth of the LORD** doth man live (Deuteronomy 8:3).

Jesus responded with the same Word when He was tempted to turn stone into bread. Jesus used the written Word to overcome every time, and then He declared we can take courage because He overcame the dark world. How did He do it? By faith in the written Word, and by that same faith He produced many miracles!

Let's understand the difference between the written and the spoken Word. It can be the same, but there are times when God speaks to His people in a practical sense as well.

Today, faith in God's written Word will bring God's power into places of corruption, evil, sickness, chaos, and every evil work which is the result of the great fall in Eden. When I believe *as the Scriptures say*, the Word of God will always do what it is written to do.

> He that believeth on me, **as the scripture hath said**, out of his belly shall flow rivers of living water (John 7:38).

A common problem among today's professing believers is that the Word is not believed *as the Scripture says*. If there are no flowing rivers coming from within, we must conclude, "I do not believe *as the Scripture says*." If, instead, belief in the Word is "as I think it says" or "as others think it says," the result is a powerless Gospel with great deficiency of demonstration of the Holy Spirit.

The extended results are a powerless church that calls sin "weaknesses" that are therefore easily tolerated by excuse. In many churches, sin is not hell-worthy anymore. "Sin" has become only a syndrome of someone's faults.

Lucifer changes sin into weaknesses or syndromes so that the poor soul finds excuses rather than repentance or deliverance. Until righteousness by faith is restored, we will not see the power of Almighty God prevail in the church.

For example, let's see what happened when Jesus and Peter did several miracles. You will see that the ones who were healed glorified God, and that is what miracles are to do.

And immediately he received his sight, and followed him, glorifying God: and all the people, when they saw it, gave praise unto God (Luke 18:43).

Then Peter said, Silver and gold have I none; but such as I have give I thee: In the name of Jesus Christ of Nazareth rise up and walk. And he took him by the right hand, and lifted him up: and immediately his feet and ankle bones received strength. And he leaping up stood, and walked, and entered with them into the temple, walking, and leaping, and praising God. And all the people saw him walking and praising God: (Acts 3:6-9).

The healing of the young man at the temple caused a stir. The religious became very upset. Peter saw this, and hear his response:

And when Peter saw it, he answered unto the people, Ye men of Israel, why marvel ye at this? or why look ye so earnestly on us, as though by **our own power or holiness** we had made this man to walk? And **his [Jesus'] name through faith in his name** hath made this man strong, whom ye see and know: yea, the faith which is by him hath given him this perfect soundness in the presence of you all (Acts 3:16).

Jesus' name and faith in His name healed the lame man. That truth never changes, nor will it ever be outdated.

Oh, the tremendous depth of dedication and unbiased surrender that it takes in the life of the believer to live in the consistency of God's truth! To live under the power of the cross is much too costly for many. The cross deals ever so harshly with the soul power of man. When this happens, the fantasizing dreams of mystical worship of the imaginary are crushed, and the sleeping saints who have need of nothing are rudely awakened.

The cross of Christ is so powerful it undoes everything that is against God or the Holy Spirit. To live in the promises of God on a continual basis is, without question, God's divine will. The true cross of Christ cannot be manipulated by man, only surrendered to without reservation. This is far more than most professing believers are willing to accept, and the excuse of misinterpretation of the Word of God becomes a convenient fallacy. As a result, the carnal man takes personal and congregational license to believe the written Word of God only in what makes comfortable the soul power of man. Believing what is convenient and counting the rest as outdated or obsolete or non-applicable is, in its simplest sense, called unbelief.

If we wonder why our life is so powerless to do the works of God, then let us consider this. If we wonder why we do not receive much revelation from the Word of God, consider this as well. We cannot put out the light and yet expect it to illuminate our hearts.

The Word of God is not given to be received or believed without the power of the cross. It is the power of the cross! If the power of the cross is not surrendered to, then the Holy Spirit, the resurrection of the dead, cannot operate with power and demonstration from heaven. And then the Word of God loses its divine authority.

In simple terms, when we speak of surrendering to the cross or making the cross practical to us today, we are referring to a surrender of our own will. The holding of our tongue instead of lashing out. The stopping of our hands that wish to beat up. The choice of grace and forgiveness instead of hate and resistance. We are willing to surrender our own will and our own selfish ways for His will and His ways.

The Holy Spirit, which is heaven's power on earth, cannot empower the spoken Word of God within an unbelieving heart. Unbelief will turn people from receiving the promises of God, even territorially (in the heavens and the earth). Unbelief can keep a whole church from operating without the power of God.

Jesus saw this at work in His home city of Nazareth. He could not do many mighty works in that town because of their unbelief.

> And he did not many mighty works there because of their unbelief (Matthew 13:58).

At times when Jesus healed someone He had to close the door between the sick and the curious. The unbelief of onlookers was a detriment to even His faith.

This has become the norm in a large majority of professors in Christ. Here we find so many that vehemently deny the will of God and His Word concerning miracles and call it all "outdated" and "non-applicable." This is personal deception and always causes the Christian to walk in darkness and powerlessness while denying truth that is never outdated.

This is why miracles are called "deception" by the multitudes. The lack of faith in the Word of God held by many does not go so far as to say there is no power to work miracles. The reason that most cannot have faith to move mountains is because they stumble in knowing the will of God. We must always know the will of God before we can pray effectively. The carnal man seeks to find agreeable things in the Word of God to fit his opinion and personal agenda. The spiritual man surrenders to any condition required by God. Doing the works of God takes the deepest humility known to mankind. Here is where many cannot stoop under the true requirements of faith and endure its consequences. Those who do have such humility will come under fire from judgmental minds.

Some of the greatest orators of God's Word have excelled in all except lowliness of mind and spirit. The astounding ability of their performance is much higher than the lowliness of the cross of Jesus. The result is a mighty "Wow is me!" instead of the sobering cry of "Woe is me!"

So much is missing in the modern message. The works of God are rarely seen in our day because faith is so masterfully analyzed that the true power of God is not in it.

Let us not forget the danger of the carnal/natural man. He cannot receive the things of the Spirit of God, because they are spiritually discerned. Let us understand this point in the Scripture. Spiritual discernment is not "figuring it all out," nor is it an intellectual ability to comprehend.

It is the ability to receive inspiration and revelation of unseen truth because it is not preconceived.

> But the natural man receiveth not the things of the Spirit of God: for they are foolishness unto him: neither can he know them, because they are spiritually discerned (1 Corinthians 2:14).

True believing always exposes the unbeliever by the power that works within the believer. We first see this with the jealousy that Cain had against Abel. He saw that God had respect for Abel's offering, yet Cain's own offering God could not receive.

The unbelieving are of carnal nature and have extreme difficulty with the substance of faith. It is too simple, and it takes a deep work of dying to self to believe all things in the written Word of God.

Jesus healed a woman who was an "Abrahamic daughter," implying that she was a believer. (Abraham is the father of all them that believe.) For eighteen years, she was bound with a sickness that kept her from walking.

> And, behold, there was a woman which had a **spirit of infirmity eighteen years**, and was **bowed together**, and could in **no wise lift up herself**. And when Jesus saw her, he called her to him, and said unto her, Woman, **thou art loosed** from thine infirmity. And he laid his hands on her: and immediately she **was made straight**, and glorified God (Luke 13:11-13).

What happens next? People became upset and blamed Jesus for healing on the Sabbath! And Jesus said to the ruler who was filled with indignation,

> And ought not this woman, being a **daughter of Abraham**, whom **Satan hath bound**, lo, these eighteen years, be **loosed from this bond** on the sabbath day? (Luke 13:16).

Sabbath was not the problem! Lucifer was the problem! He had lost his eighteen-year grip on the woman, and God was glorified.

To this very day, over two thousand years later, people who do not walk in faith but in unbelief still get upset when Satan loses his grip on the children of Abraham. The problem is a simple one to understand. Carnal man cannot have any joy in healings.

The true enemy of God always desires to dissolve and diminish the Word of God! The eternal result of taking away or adding onto the written Word is a consequence that has its start on earth.

> And if any man shall take away from the words of the book of this prophecy, God shall take **away his part out of the book of life**, and **out of the holy city**, and **from the things which are written in this book** (Revelation 22:19).

The Bible is called the book of prophecy. It forth-tells to the ones who believe as well as to the ones who do not believe. Taking away from this Bible will take away our part from the Book of Life. The first consequence is lifelessness now, on earth. The ultimate consequence is eternal lifelessness.

> He that hath the Son hath life; and he that hath not the Son of God hath not life (1 John 5:12).

You might have had the greatest experience with Christ that is possible for man, yet if you are now lifeless, you do not have the Son. Lifelessness is the result of unbelief.

Last, yet not least, is that the guilty one will be removed from the Book of Prophecy, the Holy Bible. Oh, the awful cost of unbelief!

The Bible speaks about the condition of the end-time church, when many will be offended. Satan sows tares among the wheat (i.e., church). Tares often reveal themselves by being the ones who are easily offended—it is their very nature. We must understand that tares will betray the true ones of God and will always thrive on offenses. Tares have many opinions, but the stark difference is that they have no life! A true child of the kingdom will not carry offense nor have part in betrayal, but will always find their victory in the power of the cross.

Tares do not live by faith. Their purpose is perfectionistic performance without faith and therefore they do not understand the promises of God by experience. The just shall live by faith in all the promises of God.

> For all the promises of God in him are yea, and in him Amen, unto the glory of God by us (2 Corinthians 1:20).

All the promises of God are in Jesus, yes and amen!

CHAPTER 3

Source of Faith

Where does faith come from?

My memory goes to an alcoholic I once knew. He could recite many of the New Testament books by memory, yet he was not a Christian. Faith does not come by memory, nor does it come by reading the Word.

> So then faith cometh by hearing, and hearing by the word of God (Romans 10:17).

Can a person read the word of God without hearing it? I believe it's clear that we can.

But what have I been hearing? If what I am hearing is not increasing my faith, I conclude that I am not hearing the voice of God in the Word of God. The enemy of God has handled the Word of God many times, and in ways that can tragically destroy faith. We see this in the Garden of Eden. Lucifer quoted this:

> For God doth know that in the day ye eat thereof,
> then your eyes shall be opened, and **ye shall be as
> gods**, knowing good and evil (Genesis 3:5).

God spoke this:

> And the LORD God said, Behold, the **man is
> become as one of us**, to know good and evil: and
> now, lest he put forth his hand, and take also of
> the tree of life, and eat, and live forever: (Genesis
> 3:22).

Hearing is much more important than any other human function concerning faith. If my hearing is incorrect, I can miss my destiny. Joshua and Caleb heard what God said about Canaan, but the rest of the spies heard what their eyes said about Canaan. Their ultimate destinies were eternities apart.

Hearing is often relative to the condition of what is within. The statement has often been made that you hear what you want to hear. This is not always correct, but it does carry some valid truth. I would restate that phrase as follows: A man hears according to what elements control and influence his heart.

Since the fall of Adam and Eve in the garden, man has been regulated by his soul power unless and until he surrenders to God and is then overpowered by the Holy Spirit.

Receiving the promises of God comes as a result of the spoken Word by the voice of the Spirit. The Word without the power of the Spirit is dangerous and causes the natural man to lean on his own understanding to interpret as is acceptable to him. The Word without the voice of the Spirit is as dangerous as the voice without the Word. "My sheep know my voice," Jesus declared, and the sheep know their Shepherd by His voice, sound, and personality.

The Holy Spirit is the revealer of truth.

I will be greatly affected by the Word when I read with unbiased openness to instruction, inspiration, and revelation, because then He (the Spirit) has freedom within. The Word becomes a lamp to my feet, and as a result, I will be changed to what God wills for my life.

However, if the Holy Spirit is quenched or grieved we bring His purpose to a halt.

If there is a shadow of darkness and sin within my heart, I become protective of that by the manipulations of self will. The Word will appear blurred, and my vision will be double. This prevents the Word from penetrating my heart to the point of changing me.

If I have preconceived ideas about specific doctrine in the Word, clinging to those ideas can disable me from what God is truly saying in other passages as well. I have to read the Bible with the attitude that God wants me to be changed by His revealed truth. A healthy heart is diligent to be teachable in the Word of God.

Even things I have always done by way of preconceived thoughts or traditions can overpower my soul and make the Word of God without effect when I read it. This small element of self will overrule the power of hearing and the Word of God will become of none affect.

> Making the word of God of none effect through your tradition, which ye have delivered: and many such like things do ye (Mark 7:13).

You see that my hearing can be marred deeply by my unwillingness to give myself to hear. I must surrender and hear God's way alone.

Faith comes when I start to hear correctly. Where does hearing come from? Hearing comes by the Word. This means there is powerful heavenly life in the Word of God.

Eternal power dwells within the Word. According to the Word of God, this power has the ability to give hearing to man if he is submitted to God. How does the power of the Word of God work within?

> For the word of God is quick, and powerful, and sharper than any twoedged sword, piercing even to the dividing asunder of soul and spirit, and of the joints and marrow, and is a discerner of the thoughts and intents of the heart (Hebrews 4:12).

I want to examine this verse, one of many favorites of mine.

The Word of God is quick. In Greek the word for *quick* is *zao*, meaning it is alive.

The Word of God is powerful, *energes*, which means it is active.

The Word of God is sharp, *tomoteros*, cutting with a single decisive blow.

The Word of God is piercing, *diikneomai*, penetrating without limits.

With our knowledge of the exact meanings of these original words, let us rephrase this verse for clearer understanding:

The Word of God is powerful, alive, and extremely active! It is a precise cutting device that has limitless ability to penetrate the most difficult place within man. It severs and slashes man's soulish abilities which are apart from the resident dwelling place of the Holy Spirit. It even cuts and severs man's strong natural character traits and formations of thought where soulish intentions lodge.

When the Word severs these strongholds, it puts man in a place of rest and unity with God! Now the man is completely changed and transformed from all his folly to walk differently and to think the thoughts of God. He is now spiritual, because there has been death and resurrection in his transformed heart. This is the daily walk of the saints!

If man will not hear and receive the Word, or if he even slightly deters the Word by reason or preconceived ideas, he strays farther away from the power of God. What is so awful about this condition is that unwillingness to hear becomes blindness. This blindness keeps a man in the dark about his condition without the power of God, and blindness and powerlessness become a way of life. He is now in continual defeat and excuses his own weaknesses as a way of life. This condition produces an extremely difficult realm of deception that fights against acknowledging the debauchery within because of sin's entanglement.

This blind and powerless man is now subject to the enticements of reasoning between good and evil. It is a reasoning that originates from Eden, motivated by his soul power and void of God. When God saw this dark supremacy operating within Adam and Eve, He immediately removed them from the tree of life and closed the gate to the garden.

Adam and Eve yielded to the manipulative suggestion from a fallen angel that they should exercise their own way. The serpent was in that tree of reason and knowledge. It was the seat of Satan. It is still the seat of Satan.

We find the seat of Satan again in Pergamos, where Jesus speaks from out of a two-edged sword and declares that the church has not denied the faith of Jesus.

> And to the angel of the church in Pergamos write; These things saith he which hath the **sharp sword with two edges**; I know thy works, and where thou dwellest, even where Satan's seat is: and thou holdest fast my name, and hast **not denied my faith** (Revelation 2:12-13).

I notice that Satan's seat is not far from the two-edged sword and among the bulrushes of those who hold fast to the name of Jesus and refuse to deny His faith. With these faithful ones, Satan cannot have the resident seat. He attempts to place his seat as close as he can get to those who hold fast to the faith. Satan is the defeated stranger who seeks residence near the saints of God according to his own declaration. We must never become ignorant of his devices.

In Ezekiel 28:2, God says that Lucifer even declared that he sits in the seat of God. This was Lucifer's own fall.

Thine heart was lifted up because of **thy beauty**, thou hast corrupted **thy wisdom** by reason of **thy brightness**: I will cast thee to the ground, I will lay thee before kings, that they may behold thee (Ezekiel 28:17).

When you study the fall of the archangel, you will see that with him fell one third of all other angels. Here you see three ranks in the heavens.

Lucifer saw *his own beauty*, and that *corrupted his wisdom* by reason *of his brightness*. What did Lucifer have before his fall? Beauty, wisdom, and a bright way of thinking. What did Eve have before her fall?

And when the woman **saw** that the tree was good for food, and that it was **pleasant to the eyes**, and a tree **to be desired** to make one wise, she took of the fruit thereof, and did eat, and gave also unto her husband with her; and he did eat (Genesis 3:6).

After she conversed with the fallen angel, she saw she had *beauty, wisdom*, and reasoning power of *her own brilliance*. She could use her own reasoning powers rather than trusting God's Word.

Eve now questioned God, the supreme intelligent Being of all eternity, and mistrusted what He said to them concerning the one tree. After the conversation with Lucifer, she was enticed to use her own reasoning power and judgment. She decided that what God had said was relative to her opinion.

In making a conclusion that God's Word was not important, she was completely deceived by her own judgment.

Now Adam and Eve are declared fallen and operate from their own judgment seat. Their bases of judgment are darkened, and their reasoning between good and evil is guided by notion and exterior influence upon their soul.

Everything went into a spiral of death and progressed into transcending global fallouts of curses that spread to life in all the universe, unleashing a massive flood of hell. Every child born is now subject to a condition of tragic loss and curses. The catastrophe was the biggest devastation earth's history has ever seen.

All this happened while there were only two people—and one was a son of God.

> Which was the son of Enos, which was the son of Seth, which was the son of Adam, **which was the son of God** (Luke 3:38).

This catastrophe was much greater than the flood of Noah—this was what caused the flood of Noah! When Eve turned to her own reasoning powers and was deceived, it was called the fall of humanity, and now all have sinned and come far short of God's glory.

God's glory within us is to walk in unquestionable obedience to the spoken Word of God, regardless of how unreasonable it appears to our human senses. But the soul power dominates in a fallen man without the Holy Spirit, and when man yields himself to believe by his own reason and senses, he cannot eat of the tree of life.

The only way the Holy Spirit can live within man is in the spirit of man known as the temple of the Holy Spirit. Adam and Eve's fall was so simple, yet so terribly deadly. It collapsed the spirit of man and gave room for the soul of man to exercise its human qualities. These human qualities are now sickened by a demonic influenza which causes belief to be only in that which makes sense and is visible.

The sword which is the Word of God is the only thing that divides the soul from the spirit. Until I choose the unbiased Word to pierce my difficult heart and then divide the soulish ability from the temple of God, there is no change within. All is controlled by my soulish power to perform and to show forth my own abilities.

There was an angel with a sword set at the entrance gate of Eden to keep Adam and Eve from the tree that caused man to live forever. We see the visitation of that same sword in Hebrews 4:12 again.

If you take away the letter *s* from *sword*, it becomes *Word of God*. The sword, which is the Word of God, is so powerful that God combined the Word with the Spirit from His mouth. Herein, I understand, rests the essence of faith.

We know that hearing comes by the Word of God. But where does faith come from? Faith comes by hearing. So if faith comes by hearing, we must hear first before faith comes. This is true.

Now we can see why there are so few people with great faith. My heart's constant desire and prayer is that God would deal with my heart and correct my hearing by the power of the Word, regardless of what it costs me.

✧

Have you ever met professors of Christ who were as lifeless as though there were no Jesus? This is why! They are strangers to faith.

There is a modern phrase that says, "Just believe." This is not the spiritual faith that we read about in the Bible, nor the faith that I am writing about.

> For with the heart man believeth unto righteousness; and with the mouth confession is made unto salvation (Romans 10:10).

Following the Word without the Spirit will not give you life. The quickening Spirit of God gives life, as He did in the resurrection of Jesus when He gave life to the entombed body of Christ after three days of death. Paul wept as he wrote that there are many who live as the enemies of the true cross of Christ (Philippians 3:18). This is because they refuse to hear correctly. They have not allowed the death of the cross to come upon their preconceptions and mechanisms of hearing. Their hearing is tainted, and this is why there are no signs that follow them in their professed belief. There is never a shortcut in the way of the cross, and without taking up the cross daily, man will never become a disciple.

The Holy Spirit is a quickening Spirit, giving life through spiritual resurrection. We see this *quickening* in the beginning of creation.

> In the beginning God created the heaven and the earth. And the earth was without form, and void; and darkness was upon the face of the deep. And the Spirit of God moved upon the face of the waters (Genesis 1:1-2).

God saw the earth was dark, void, and formless. All was in chaos. The Spirit of God moved over the waters. God moved His mouth, and spiritual currents of air formed words that came forth.

When you look at the word *Spirit* in Greek and Hebrew, the meaning is *a current of air*. So the Holy Spirit is a Holy Current of breath and functions as a person.

All this flowed out of God and caused all to become as He spoke. This is called *the Word*. The Word is extremely powerful because of its origin. *The mixing of the Word of God with faith within the believer, moved by the Holy Spirit, gives full release to do what it is promised to do.* This spiritual phenomenon causes power beyond human ability.

This is called faith.

This is what Almighty God is looking for in order to put into effect His supernatural power.

> And what is the exceeding greatness of his power to us-ward who believe, according to the working of his mighty power (Ephesians 1:19).

It is substance of things that I hope for, but the invisible evidence is seen alone in God's Word.

God has given us this truth to do His will on earth according to His Word. God alone is immensely glorified when someone surrenders and has spiritual faith. This pleases Him. If my hearing is correct and open before God, I will then have a spiritual faith. What is the purpose of faith then in my life? It is the only means that is acceptable before God for man to live by.

> The just shall live by faith (Hebrews 10:38).

> Christ dwells in our hearts by faith (Ephesians 3:17).

> For ye are all children of God by faith (Galatians 3:26).

> For we walk by faith and not by sight (2 Corinthians 5:7).

> By whom also ye have access by faith into this grace (Romans 5:2).

The promises of God are all made available for God's children to walk in, by the empowerment of the Word by the Holy Spirit. Let us not forget not that without faith, the promises will not be received and God is not glorified, because without faith it is impossible to please God.

> For unto us was the gospel preached, as well as unto them: but the **word preached** did not profit them, not being **mixed with faith** in them that heard it (Hebrews 4:2).

How then is the Word mixed with faith? According to this reference, you can hear the Word and not mix it with faith, and then it will profit you nothing. But if you hear the Word and accept it as a promise and gift from God, without question or doubt, it will profit what it was spoken to do.

Many well-meaning, carnal men say that the original Word of God, as it is written, "is not for me." That is exactly right! It is not for carnal man. Others, still farther away, say the Word of God is for no one at all in our day.

Let us learn from those who have had faith and saw results in the mighty works of God for His glory alone.

As I have noted before, this faith is not a lifestyle or set of rules. It is faith that God can work through to perform His promises to mankind.

If things are possible for mankind to do, then it does not take faith to do them. Therefore, this is not what God is speaking about. Faith is to move mountains and stop the mouth of the lion (2 Timothy 4:17).

These people of faith are hated people and are not well spoken of by the majority. But they are the obedient, human vessels operating by the power of God within, operating as kings and priests on the earth. They hear the Word and act upon it by faith.

> Who through faith subdued kingdoms, wrought righteousness, obtained promises, stopped the mouths of lions. Quenched the violence of fire, escaped the edge of the sword, out of weakness were made strong, waxed valiant in fight, turned to flight the armies of the aliens (Hebrews 11:33-34).

I recognize I am not on earth for myself, but completely for the purpose of Christ, even if it causes carnal man to hate me and speak all manner of things against me falsely. Christ has called me to have a living faith that carries the power of God for His glory.

So where exactly is the Word, and what precisely is the Word?

> In the beginning was the Word, and the Word was with God, and the Word was God (John 1:1).

The Word was with God at the creation, because God was the Word. When God told Adam and Eve not to eat, that was God who spoke it, and He was and is the Word. Jesus is called the Word as well.

> And to make all men see what is the fellowship of the mystery, which from the beginning of the world hath been hid in God, who created all things by Jesus Christ: (Ephesians 3:9).

God created all things by the Word. Jesus is the Word, and God was the Word spoken by the Holy Spirit.

> And the Word was made flesh, and dwelt among us, (and we beheld his glory, the glory as of the only begotten of the Father,) full of grace and truth (John 1:14).

So we see that the Word was the creator and was God. The creator was also Jesus. Jesus spoke by the empowerment of the Holy Ghost, and it was so. When all of the Godhead speaks, it is so!

God said. Jesus said. The Holy Spirit said.

Now what do I say?

This is where I find faith that moves mountains, which I will address later. This is my purpose for writing this book.

Now may our faith allow Him to do all of that which He spoke, and it will become what He hath spoken. And it will be so!

> And God said, Let there be light: and there was light (Genesis 1:3).

The only thing that can withhold the Word from becoming what is intended is the naturally poisoned, soulish power which is called unbelief.

> And **all things, whatsoever ye shall ask in prayer, believing, ye shall receive** (Matthew 21:22).

Do I still believe the Word of God?

> And in that day ye shall ask me nothing. Verily, verily, I say unto you, **Whatsoever ye shall ask the Father in my name, he will give it you. Hitherto have ye asked nothing in my name: ask, and ye shall receive, that your joy may be full** (John 16:23-24).

May I ask again: Do I still believe the Word of God?

Can you sense that the soulish man does not by nature like this? Why not? He cannot have faith because he refuses to hear. And right here is where Abram became Abraham and fell upon his face and laughed. He saw it! He saw the invisible evidence! And after he saw this truth, within a year he had a miracle son, Isaac.

Many are stuck in a certain persuasion of religion and therefore are not willing to hear the Word with complete clarity for fear they might have to change. I have no present experiential understanding of such rebellion against the Word of God. Nor do I go to the Word to settle an argument. I go to the Word unbiased and open to being changed and transformed—and then I can hear the Word of God. This is God's way of leading me by His Spirit and through His Word into greater depths of His truth.

I want to give an example. I will ask you to simply read and see what happens within your heart as you read. Be honest as to what is going on deep within as you read this verse spoken by God, by Jesus, and by the Holy Spirit, through Paul.

> Who his own self bare our sins in his own body
> on the tree, that we, being dead to sins, should
> live unto righteousness: by whose stripes ye **were
> healed** (1 Peter 2:24).

Did this make you defensive or was there an inner rejoicing?

The part that makes carnal man uncomfortable is the last part of the verse. Why so? Because without faith, we cannot believe the true meaning of this verse, and faith is a stretch for the carnal man. He cannot receive this truth because he is dominated by soul power.

By whose stripes ye were healed! Here the word *stripes* means *blow-marks*. Jesus was flogged, and deep marks were left in His flesh. The blood flowed from the wounds and inflicted a slow death upon Him. Here it says that we *were* (past tense) healed by those blows in Pilate's courtyard that night.

Quickly, the natural man will say, "Oh, that is nothing special." His conclusion is that these words simply mean inner healing from sin. Here the carnal man has certainly joined the world system of believing in all sorts of healing—except for physical healing.

Friend, sin does not get healed. Sin needs to be forgiven through Jesus' death on the cross as a substitute for us. There was a price of death to pay for our sin. Did our sickness demand the same death penalty?

Jesus took all sin, sickness, and curses into the grave and rose again by the Holy Spirit's power. So is the Word of God saying that real sicknesses were healed at the cross?

This is what the Scripture says: "by whose stripes ye *were* healed." In the Bible, healing is always in reference to physical sickness—and nothing has changed for today.

If we think "sickness" can be replaced by "sin" or that the two can be used interchangeably, try exchanging *sin* for *sickness* and the error will become obvious. For example, "When we confess our sickness, He is just and faithful to forgive our sickness." This is in error. Here is another example, the other way around. "The prayer of faith shall save the sinful." This is wrong again.

Why is it so difficult to believe exactly what the Scriptures say?

What is going through our hearts by now? Let us discern what our hearts are prone to believe. Ask, *How am I hearing this?* Is there a preconceived idea that sits comfortably within and guards everything that needs the cross of faith?

I have seen many people receive their healing once they believed what the Scripture says, the way it says. They saw that it happened in the work of the cross and resurrection from the dead. When I believe *as the Scripture says*, then—and only then—is when the river waters flow from deep within.

> He that believeth on me, **as the scripture hath said, out of his belly shall flow rivers of living water** (John 7:38).

In this latter day, you will see a prevalence of opinion that says faith is unrelated to truth. There are many who refuse to believe as the Scripture hath said. The result is dry, powerless lives that have no flowing rivers of living water. This is a result of how we hear.

> Take heed therefore how ye hear: for whosoever hath, to him shall be given; and whosoever hath not, from him shall be taken even that which he seemeth to have (Luke 8:18).

We are instructed to take heed how we hear. Let us look at ourselves for a moment. How do I hear? Do I require evidence seen by my eyes before I can hear? Do I require understanding that matches my own opinion before I hear?

No, I hear because it is the Word of God, even if it is not understood. In His time, He gives us understanding. I am to believe the Word, because the Word is Christ. So depending how I hear, I will be given much more—or lose everything that I seemed to have had at one time. Hearing is very important to having faith in God's sovereign promises to the redeemed.

The problem is that we think hearing is not important—and that it is even optional. But hearing is very important to having faith in God's sovereign promises to the redeemed.

"Oh ye of little faith"

What does God say about "little faith," and how do we overcome it?

We want to examine what Jesus said about little faith in specific incidents in the Gospels.

Let us look at the context of the first reference to little faith.

Jesus was teaching about not doing things for the purpose of being seen by man—like giving alms openly and making long prayers in public. He said praying should be in the closet, where none but the Father sees.

Jesus clearly taught not to pray repeated prayers, and I find it interesting that right after He said this, He gave us an example of a prayer known as the Lord's Prayer. This prayer should also not be a prayer of repetitive praying. The very thing that Jesus said not to do is done all the time, especially in Catholicism.

However, the pivotal point of His teaching in this passage is as follows.

> For where your treasure is, there will your heart be also. The light of the body is the eye: if therefore thine eye be single, thy whole body shall be full of light. But if thine eye be evil, thy whole body shall be full of darkness. If therefore the light that is in thee be darkness, how great is that darkness! (Matthew 6:21-23)

I want to address the subject of a "single eye."

If my one eye focuses on one thing and my other eye focuses on another subject at the same time, I cannot see anything clearly. This is how many Christians try to live. This is how many read the Holy Bible. One eye is on tradition or culture, which they secretly love or are controlled by. The other eye is on the Word. One eye is in the world, the other in the Word.

If we would try to pilot a plane in this way, we would have a certain crash. If we read our Bible this way, we will always be seeking for life and truth, but we'll seldom find it.

When we read with double vision, it also becomes a dreaded duty, because we will have the illusion of two masters.

> No man can serve two masters: for either he will hate the one, and love the other; or else he will hold to the one, and despise the other. Ye cannot serve God and mammon (Matthew 6:24).

Multitudes try to be a child of God, hoping that God will somehow supply their needs. God's instruction is simple: Seek God's kingdom first with singleness of eye, and all these things shall be added unto you. Let both eyes focus on God's entire kingdom, and that will illuminate the entire body.

> The light of the body is the eye: if therefore thine eye be single, thy whole body shall be full of light (Matthew 6:22).

If you have two subjects of focus, that is called an evil eye. We have to come to a place of singularly focused dependence on Christ and His promises to us. We must have a change of heart to be in single focus on what His Word says. The doubled-eyed man is unstable in all his ways, and he can be assured that he will not receive from the Lord.

> But let him ask **in faith, nothing wavering**. For he that wavereth is like a wave of the sea driven with the wind and tossed. For **let not that man think that he shall receive any thing of the Lord**. A double minded man is unstable in all his ways (James 1:6-8).

This is speaking about double mindedness and double vision, and the result is wavering faith or little faith. This man will receive nothing from the Lord. When I waver in my faith, it shuts up the heavens from my life. The instruction is quite clear:

> (For after all these things do the Gentiles seek:) for your heavenly Father knoweth that ye have need of all these things. But seek ye first the kingdom of God, and his righteousness; and all these things shall be added unto you (Matthew 6:32-33).

Truly this is what Jesus says. With eyes that know and see eternity in clarity, this truth becomes foundational to all eternity and is filled with heavenly glory, because it takes us there!

This is also the context of Jesus' words about the lovely lily, declaring that all the glory of King Solomon was nothing compared to being arrayed like the lilies of the field.

King Solomon was as wealthy as a man could be in his day. He owned golden chariots and palaces, and he built a multibillion-dollar temple. That was nothing in comparison to the garb of the lily? This is what Jesus said when He compared the two.

How can I understand this comparison and arrive at the same conclusion?

The lily known as *shoshan* was a white lily that still grows in Galilee and on Mt. Carmel. The flower of the lily lives about five days and is spread open day and night. At night, the lily becomes more fragrant. A dirty lily is something rarely seen, and in the Christian era, this lily is symbolic of spiritual purity, holiness, and resurrection. The lily does not toil or spin. It does not concern itself whether or not it rains. If there is rain, it drinks, and if there is no rain, it draws water from its roots.

Simple trust is the equivalent of water for the lily, regardless of which way it comes. When it rains, you drink; and if it does not, you adjust and draw from the roots. The root system is the invisible strength within a true child of God.

Roots are sent much deeper in drought conditions. The root system is to grow into the spoken/written Word of God. The purpose of dry epochs is to establish the root system in a spiritual man. This is exactly what Israel was to endure in the Sinai desert for forty years. What happens within the carnal man through these memorable seasons of testing is a picture of complaint, discouragement, and even anger. But the spiritual man draws from the roots, never becomes discouraged, and rests assured in the promises of God. Therefore, the life of the lily becomes queen in the desert!

The great King Solomon never had what a true, born-again believer has if he trusts in the Lord. So what is the glory of the saint compared to the riches of the richest man on earth?

The greatest truth of the lily is a simple one: It does not have to work to become a lily—it is one indeed! Solomon had to toil and get all he could to become what he was. The lily does not have to struggle to become a lily—it is simply a lily.

When you are a true child of God, you are just that. You don't have to toil to become His child, even though many do. The carnal man "has to" be a Christian. He will try hard to do just what he needs to do to appear as one. The carnal man has to prove to God and himself and others that he is a Christian. The spiritual man is a Christian because the Word has spoken so! He does not have to spin and toil to become what God said He is!

A castaway is someone who easily excels in knowledge about God but has not paid the price of personal experience.

The wonderful truth about the lily is that it presents the promise of being what God has imputed—without toil. When the child of God humbles himself and accepts what God has declared, it is much more glorious than all the self-work that Solomon could achieve.

And yet I say unto you, That even Solomon in all his glory was not arrayed like one of these. Wherefore, if God so clothe the grass of the field, which to day is, and to morrow is cast into the oven, shall he not much more clothe you, **O ye of little faith?** (Matthew 6:29-30)

Herein lies truth. This is what happens by faith. We will become who we are in Him, if we allow ourselves to become who He is. This is the lily! I am in Him and He is in me. I am speaking about those who have truly given their life to Christ, with deep repentance from their own way, and now live an unbiased life before Almighty God. So many Christians are always trying to "become," and as a result never accept who they *are* in Christ. If you are in Christ, you are a new creation. The Bible does not say that if you are in Christ you will "try to become" a new creation.

I give the example of two kittens. They were twins and snow white. One was filthy, dirty, muddy, bloody from a fight, and carrying an awful stench because of where it dwelled. The other was as clean as can be, with a fluffy and healthy white coat.

When I ask Christians which kitten best describes themselves, the answer is astounding. Most will shamefully, even tearfully, admit they are the dirty one.

Now bring the two kittens to me as I place them on a ledge between a muddy and filthy barnyard on one side and, on the other side, a clean, warm, carpeted room with a fireplace burning in a serene environment.

When I release both kittens, which way do you think the two will run? You already know the answer.

As long as you do not accept what God says about who you are in Christ, you will find your tendencies keep you away from Christ and under continual guilt. To become a true saint of God, we must humbly acknowledge who God declares us to be as Christians. All else is the sin of unbelief!

If I "try" to be what God says I am, I will never become what God wants me to be, because it is *me trying* to become. And lilies are what lilies are. They are what they are intended to be, and herein we find rest as the children of God.

> There remaineth therefore a rest to the people of God. For he that is entered into his rest, he also hath ceased from his own works, as God did from his. Let us labour therefore to enter into that rest, lest any man fall after the same example of unbelief (Hebrews 4:9-11).

This rest is received by faith in what God says. When you seek first the kingdom of God, He will add all these things to you as His child.

Some Christians make statements of faith concerning seeking first the kingdom of God and expect results in the next hour or the same day. It does not usually work this way.

Patience is a kingdom virtue, and this "adding unto you" takes time and process. Once your track record before God is proven by patience and trust that has become non-wavering, in His time He will fulfill His promise in a form of grace.

Here again, this grace is not earned but is given as a gift from God. Before God blesses with grace, the conditions have to be according to His requirements. The clearest way I can present the condition of His requirements is: patience, brokenness, humility, surrender, and dependence on every Word that proceeds out of the mouth of God, in the fear of God.

What is a kingdom seeker? The Bible is clear that the kingdom of God is within. Most are concerned that things *without* get proper attention. I must be aware of and welcome God's desire to do His absolute work *within*. I must—on a continual basis—give God my entire life and all that I am .

He has to perfect me into His fullness and grace so that His kingdom power is effective and facilitates His marvelous works. The functioning of the kingdom of God in this context is God doing His kingly work within me, in every corner of my life.

If my soulish nature is not fully surrendered to Christ, I become a castaway. A castaway is someone who easily excels in knowledge *about* God but has not paid the price of personal experience. These are among the most difficult people on earth. They are frustrated because they know the answer to everyone's problem, yet they walk in confidence that has no power. These people seemingly do well and need no faith—until they discover their personal condition has a root source far from God. Within, they are knotted up with a critical heart filled with mistrust, and they lack the grace of God upon themselves as well as grace toward others. They focus on control and intimidation through anemic friendships by lifting up those whom they want to impress, and if this fails, they make others their enemy. These are they of little faith.

There might be an expression of self-importance, whatever that might be. The destruction of such a weighty problem within the heart is what the Holy Spirit led Christ through.

The answer for this condition is spiritual obedience. How is spiritual obedience learned? By learning obedience through things that we suffer for the kingdom of God! The Son of Almighty God learned it this way.

> Though he were a Son, yet learned he obedience by the things which he suffered; And being made perfect, he became the author of eternal salvation unto all them that obey him (Hebrews 5:8-9).

Spiritual obedience comes from learning through the sufferings as a child of God. There are many who pride themselves on obedience and achievement through soul power and false burdens of piety. There is very little faith found in the shallow experience of a life that constantly steers away from the cross of Christ.

When you suffer, what do you learn? Does it bring surrender, humility, submission to Christ and to His Word? Only in this will you attain spiritual obedience, which is not obedience to a set of personal or institutional rules. You do not have to know Christ in order to obey man's requirements.

✧

We hear Jesus referring to little faith during a storm on the Sea of Galilee. Jesus entered into a ship and His disciples followed Him. As the ship left the little port on one side of Galilee, a mighty wind came up.

I have traveled through Israel on numerous occasions, and according to my understanding, during the month of May and October there are deep tropospheric disturbances that can occur in the area of the Sea of Galilee. These east winds, known as *sharqiya*, are sudden, severe, and furious. These winds blow from the east—the direction in which Jesus and His disciples were headed. They were on the way to the east bank of the Sea of Galilee, which is the country of the Gergesenes.

At once the ship was covered with the waves, and the disciples were very afraid. Did they really think God would allow the drowning of Jesus if the boat would fail them? Did they forget who invited them to follow Him into the ship?

You see here the basis of faith. When Jesus said, "Follow me," and they did, they were then under His authority, and therefore He was responsible for them.

However, there was one problem: Jesus was asleep. He was in the lower part of the boat, where He would have been the first to drown, because water flows down. He was not fearful; He was filled with faith. But He was asleep. And that was the test for the disciples.

When we see the whole picture, we understand that the storm from the east was an ambush. You see, the Holy Spirit was leading them to the other side of the sea to deal with two devil-possessed men. Do you think perhaps the devils knew that their time was nearing and that they would be cast out? I would certainly believe so, and that's why the winds came up quickly.

Will you say here that God was in charge of the winds? If so, how could Jesus rebuke the winds? If God caused the strong winds, then Jesus would not have rebuked them, or He would have been rebuking God.

> And he saith unto them, Why are ye fearful, **O ye of little faith?** Then he arose, and rebuked the winds and the sea; and there was a great calm (Matthew 8:26).

Jesus rebuked the winds and the sea, and all was calm. Then they came to the other side and met these men of the tombs. Jesus cast out the devils, and the pigs went straight for the sea that Jesus had just calmed by rebuke.

Jesus walked in the Holy Spirit and was led to do the work of God. As the enemy tried to hold them back from entering the country of the Gergesenes to deal with the devils, Jesus brought order to the mission.

When we are led by the Spirit to do the works of God, we must never fear or give in to little faith, lest we become disoriented and miss our purpose. There are many deep, sorrowful trials we must endure that are devastating, but we must hang on to eternal life and wait out the storm till it passes by. This enduring can be quite long and difficult. But if we have answered His call to follow Him, then we are under His authority and He is responsible for us. Remember, "Consider the lily!"

✧

Jesus had just fed the 5,000 men plus women and children and sent them away. He told His disciples to get into the ship and go before Him to the other side of the Sea of Galilee. They did so, and Jesus went up to a mountain to pray. Perhaps He went to the mountain of Arbel, which is the only mountain close by.

When evening came and He was alone on the mountain, He saw their ship out in the middle of the sea, which could be about three to four miles out. The waves were terrible, and the boat was battered and beaten by the storm.

Around 3:00 am, which is the fourth watch of the night, the disciples saw someone walking on the water. They thought it was a ghost. It scared them so much, they screamed with fear.

It was Jesus walking past them, heading for the other side as well. When Jesus saw and heard them, He immediately spoke to them and said, "Be of good cheer, it is I, be not afraid."

Peter said, "If this is you, Lord, ask me to come."

Jesus said, "Come."

Jesus gave Peter authority to walk on His Word. The Word was *Come*. Here we see that it does not say that the waves or water were boisterous. It says the wind was boisterous, and Peter saw this. I believe that the conditions around Jesus were perfectly smooth, and the howling winds had no effect on the water touched by the soles of His feet.

Peter stepped onto the water and started walking. As long as his walking was on the Word *Come*, all was well. But when Peter saw the winds boisterous, it got the attention of his other eye, and he began to sink. He cried, "Lord save me!"

And immediately Jesus stretched forth his hand, and caught him, and said unto him, **O thou of little faith**, wherefore didst thou doubt? (Matthew 14:31)

I consider this picture in my personal life, and what moves me is this: Do I walk according to the wind or on Jesus' word *Come?*

When Peter acknowledged the boisterous wind, he lost the place on which he had been walking. Attention to the wind sank Peter. When God gives you His will to walk on, keep your eyes on His will. Don't worry about all the commotion that surrounds it, just walk on that which He gave you to do by faith.

There are many opportunities to look at the source of commotions surrounding us in troubling times and conditions. But that is not where we are called to walk. We are called to keep our feet where God orders them to walk, whether it is on a sea of water or through impossible circumstances. Our eyes will be focused only on our Commander, because we are under His authority.

But if we have little faith and we doubt like Peter did, we will not gain any progress.

However, the Lord stretched His hand forth and Peter was brought back up.

Notice the test of faith. The winds ceased once Peter was in the boat alongside Jesus. Whether on the sea or in the ship, we are secure by His side, but we will sink every time if we allow ourselves to be distracted from His Word and voice.

Note that Jesus did not rebuke the waves. He rebuked the winds, which was the source of the waves. Man often rebukes the waves and even fails to see the wind, which is in fact the cause, and thus misses the opportunity to address the issue at the root.

And finally, notice this of great significance. When the winds were extreme and the waves were severe and darkness was the darkest, even Jesus' own disciples thought Jesus to be a ghost and an opponent force that looked evil in the middle of the storm.

With darkness, extreme wind, and deathly waves of trials and tests, even with Jesus in view, the storm can change our perception of our loving leader and master, Jesus. Jesus is never a ghost, nor an enemy to His own, regardless of how circumstances might cause Him to appear. Let the storm never change our perception of our master!

The last example I want to use is the incident after Jesus fed the four thousand. I will paraphrase the record of the events that begin in Matthew 15.

Jesus came up "into a mountain" close to the Sea of Galilee. Multitudes came, bringing with them lame, blind, dumb, maimed, and many others and "cast them down at Jesus' feet." He healed all of them.

The multitude wondered in awe when they heard the dumb speak and saw the maimed made whole and the lame to walk and the blind to see. They glorified the God of Israel in ways not seen before. This was a marvelous event! Can

Roots are sent much deeper in drought conditions.

you imagine the land full of joyful people? People who thought they could never walk again or ever see again were now jumping and dancing around in marvelous fashion, glorifying God before all of heaven and the world to see.

This went for hours and hours and lasted, in fact, for three days—and all without food. Jesus felt compassion for the hungry people and desired to feed them, lest they faint from fasting before He sent them back to their dwellings. But the disciples asked, "How can we find this much bread in the wilderness?"

All that was available was seven loaves of bread and a few fish. Jesus commanded every person to sit down on the ground. There were 4,000 men plus women and children. This could easily have been over 10,000 people.

Jesus gave thanks and broke the bread and gave it to the disciples. They gave it to the multitude. All ate and were filled.

Now Jesus, with some disciples, left the place and went to the port of Magdala, which is on the west side of the Sea of Galilee, next to Mount Arbel. Upon their arrival, the Pharisees and the Sadducees came to tempt Jesus, asking Him to show some signs from heaven.

Jesus said, "If the sky is red in the evening, you say there will be fair weather. If the sunrise is red and overcast, you say there will be rain or a storm brewing." Then He said, "You hypocrites! How is it that you can discern the face of the weather but cannot discern the signs of these times?"

May I further say, "You know the law and the prophets and know full well that the Messiah will come, and now when He is here, you are blinded and cannot see because you think He is not quite what you reasoned the Messiah to be. You look at His face and think He is no King because He has no palace and not even a stone to lay His head upon. So you refuse Him! Are not the works I do and the power that I demonstrate a sign that I am the Christ?"

Jesus went on, "A wicked and adulterous generation is a sign-seeking generation." Why? Because they cannot believe by faith. "I will give you only one sign!" said Jesus to the Pharisees. "I give you the sign of Jonas!"

What is the Jonas sign? The sign of Jonas was this: "If you see me in the belly of the earth for three days and three nights, then I have confirmed what the prophets have spoken about me—that I am the true one. The Messiah! This is what sets me apart from all the rest. I am the resurrection from the dead, and in me alone you can have the same eternal life that I have."

In other words, the evidence was not in signs and wonders, but in resurrection from the dead.

Here is the same evidence I spoke of earlier, concerning lice brought from dust. In the end time, there will be miracle workers from both sides and non-miracle workers from the same professions. The test and the evidence will not be in the miracles. It will all be in the monumental truth found in 1 John 5:12: Do you have life (*quickening power*)? Then you have Jesus. Do you not have life? Then you do not have Jesus.

What is quickening power? This heavenly power comes from the true Holy Spirit! This power will have God's nature of holiness because it is the Holy Spirit. The Holy Spirit's true resurrection power from heaven is never manipulated by the craftiness of man through impressive strategies and formulas. The quickening power of Jesus is what causes the miraculous to occur.

The Pharisees and the Sadducees wanted to see signs. They did not care about the holiness of God. In the last day, we will see men just like them. Because of their corrupt nature, they want to see signs, and yet they scorn concern for the holiness of God.

Another type of unbeliever wants to see holiness and is offended when signs follow.

You see, we must understand that signs follow those who believe. Signs follow the true believer because they are not primary in the believer's faith. If it is all about signs, then Jesus is not the primary person we follow. But if signs do not follow my life, than I must draw the tragic scriptural conclusion that I am not a true believer.

God's power within man through the Holy Spirit can do exceedingly more than I can ask or even think. But it is all based on the power that works in me.

> Now unto him that is able to do exceeding abundantly above all that we ask or think, according to the power that worketh in us (Ephesians 3:20).

If I have unbelief, I will not see the power of faith work the works of God through my life. Furthermore, I will then conclude that the power of true faith is not for our day. That conclusion makes me look good, so that I will not be in a questionable category among the multitude. However, this will place me into the perfect description of the faithless generation with leaven of the Pharisees.

> The only time there is danger is when we are out of the will of God.

There must have been so much excitement that the disciples forgot to eat bread and fish themselves as they were distributing it. Jesus had just encountered the Pharisees and Sadducees and was speaking to the disciples afterward when He said, "Take heed and be aware of the leaven of the Pharisees and Sadducees."

They heard His Word but wondered what He meant. "Was it because of us not taking bread in the midst of the miracle on the other side?"

> Which when Jesus perceived, he said unto them, **O ye of little faith**, why reason ye among yourselves, because ye have brought no bread? Do ye not yet understand, neither remember the five loaves of the five thousand, and how many baskets ye took up? Neither the seven loaves of the four thousand, and how many baskets ye took up? (Matthew 16:8-10)

Jesus said, "Don't you remember or understand the miracle and all that was left after the feeding of thousands? Oh ye of little faith. What do you think that I was speaking about? I was not speaking to you about kingdom leaven in the bread. I was warning you about the other leaven that is in the heart of two sects of reason, the doctrine of the Pharisees and Sadducees."

> How is it that ye do not understand that I spake it not to you concerning bread, that ye should beware of the leaven of the Pharisees and of the Sadducees? (Matthew 16:11)

What works in me? Faith, or the leaven of unbelief?

Let us now conclude what Jesus meant when He said, "Oh ye of little faith," and remind ourselves how we can overcome little faith.

Let us understand that the flower on the lily is there because it is a lily plant. When we are truly kingdom saints, we are cared for. Have faith in God with a single eye, not doubting.

The storm came up while Jesus was sleeping in the boat. The disciples were fearfully looking at the circumstances. They should have recognized that they were exactly where Jesus told them to be and had no need to fear. If we are where Jesus asks us to be, we can be confident, and we do not need to fear, even when it seems Jesus is sleeping. Jesus was sleeping because He saw no danger in the terrible storm. The only time there is danger is when we are out of the will of God and looking at impossible circumstances, it is then that we are of little faith.

Peter was called to come to Jesus on the water when the seas were very rough. The disciples were in a boat, fearful, and Jesus was passing by on the water without a boat and without fear. He walked in faith, and when you do so by His Word, you need never fear. When you have little faith, you can be in a seemingly safer place (like a boat) and have terrible fear.

Peter started sinking when he realized the boisterous winds about him. He lost view of the master of the wind, and then the wind became his master. He sank, and then Jesus became his master again. Sometimes sinking in little faith results in finding the real Master, and He becomes our refuge and harbor regardless of the wind.

After His disciples didn't take bread in the midst of the miracles of feeding the thousands, Jesus reminded them that what He did once has no repetitive limits. Always be aware of the leaven of reason. Faith stands no chance when manipulated by human reason.

Notice all the incidents we have spoken of concerning little faith. Each instance of "little faith" occurred in the same environment where miracles were done.

The faith that is necessary to please God will do as Jesus did when He walked among men.

Is there a call upon our lives to bring glory to God? What does God call for His glory?

> Verily, verily, I say unto you, He that believeth on me, the works that I do shall he do also; and greater works than these shall he do; because I go unto my Father. And whatsoever ye shall ask in my name, that will I do, that the Father may be glorified in the Son (John 14:12-13).

God longs to see His children walk in faith so strong that He alone gets glorified.

Faith has not changed. The place has not changed. The power has not changed. And the mission has not changed. Who has changed?

This brief study barely touches the depth of the subject of spiritual faith. The depth of greater faith is much simpler than I have had the ability to write. This is why it appears so complex as we try to understand it with reason and logic. The problem is a simple one: It is called faith!

CHAPTER 4

Purpose of Faith

Adam was created perfect—until God allowed the mouth of a serpent to test him by a reasonable suggestion from his wife. In this confrontation, the serpent cast doubt on the validity of God's spoken Word.

In this testing, Adam completely failed. Here is where Adam and Eve became imperfect and exceedingly sinful. The suggestion that seemed so trifling at the moment of temptation became the sin that destroyed their entire fellowship with God in a moment.

Man was never to be the same again. Adam and Eve had now imposed sin upon the future of every person born of a human father. Hereafter, all mankind would naturally stray from God's original intentions.

Almighty God would have to bring forth a way of redemption for all affected human beings. God did so in Christ, the true Messiah for the vast sea of sin-dominated humans. This provision now brings the individual man back into true fellowship with Almighty God through the Holy Spirit. Man can now again find God's will and purpose for his or her life.

After man confesses true spiritual repentance from his own way, he is welcomed into the will of God, and God can now convey His own sovereign ways within the consecrated man who is dedicated to God's purposes by faith.

Ancient holy men of God, through unpopular obedience and by faith, spoke prophetic words that introduced the plan of God's fulfillment within man, nations, kingdoms, and the whole world. God laid foundations of His will throughout the entire Old and New Testaments, and some prophetic words are yet to be fulfilled at the sunset of this age.

God uses different ways to bring man into His will. His method of direction to mankind is the written Word of God. He uses other means as well to bring fulfillment by His Word in more personal ways.

He uses the lips of man to lay forth personal direction, congressional direction, national direction, and even global direction. God often speaks through prophetic means, as He did in Joseph's dreams.

To reveal His truth, He often uses ways that are most confounding to human reason. In His way, He confounds the "wise." The wise are those who have figured it all out but whose imaginations and opinions have categorically missed the whole foundation of knowledge and truth. This is the only foundation that has been laid in Christ to fulfill the entire will of God within mankind.

The Holy Spirit's unveiling of His will in a personal way often comes by deep surrender and consecration within the heart. For God to secure His will within requires the most difficult virtue—one that even a spiritual man finds challenging. Patience is the virtue in which most anxious souls fail to endure. The price of this truth is hardly ever borne, because the suffering is often too misunderstood and religiously fatal.

God diminishes the power of His man to the point where there is very little left of man, so that God's power alone can fulfill His purposes through His earthen vessel. God does not do this as punishment to the old nature, but uses His earthen vessels as channels through which He imputes the new nature of righteousness by faith.

My heart is deeply moved by the pioneers of faith as they have walked before God in reverence in difficult times throughout kingdom history. These vessels of God were diminished to extreme weakness through intense difficulty in personal transformation. This was in order to make space for the heart of God to decree, through them, heaven's purpose.

To carry such power of spiritual usefulness, man has to walk in a condition that does not come from human nature. The natural man has such grand capabilities of doing many things by himself that to the eyes of self the dependence on the Holy Spirit becomes a deficit and dearth within. When man is in this self-powered condition, Holy God will never be able to perform His true desire within man or the world.

To come to the place where my own strength does not carry me anymore is far lower than most people would ever dare to go. This transformation comes alone in reverence to God Adonai and God El-Shaddai.

Until I have been carried through the valleys of the shadows of spiritual and even physical death, there remains in me the subtle ability to do all things, yet without the power of the Holy Spirit. The power of my self-man has to be torn from the throne of self-ability, come to complete emptiness, and face man's disapproval before my life will ever completely rest in His.

When my life does not rest in His, mine will be a ministry tarnished in well-meaning, like the offering sweat of Cain. Almighty God does not want me to do His work without His divine empowerment, because this affords no heavenly seal. God is not glorified in what I can do; He is glorified in what He can do through my weakness. I must stand aside and live by faith in His promises. If I will not heed the promises but pursue by my own strength, then I will be the one who does everything and thereby limiting the power of God.

When I did it, God did not. This life-changing truth was an obvious confession in Christ. This is why the believer needs to wait in the upper room till he has been endued with power from on high.

The desperation and longing has to be great and endured with much tenderness and hunger and thirst after God's promise of Pentecost.

> For the promise is unto you, and to your children, and to all that are afar off, even as many as the Lord our God shall call (Acts 2:39).

Pentecost is the only way provided whereby man can come to a place of resting his flesh from the strength of his own power. Our own power has to be proven wrong to receive this valiant anointing.

I can greatly appreciate the cry from the hearts of some who fulfill self-repressive duties for God, duties which appear impressive to the natural mind yet are unnoticed by heaven. I have heard the passionate cry of deep desire from the lives of many believers asking, "What can I do to please God? Would the mission field fulfill my cry? Would neglecting of my life's mortal man find fulfillment in God? Would voluntary poverty fulfill my cry for spiritual richness?"

May we clearly understand: Christ has become all of that, so I can walk in His blessing. The complete richness is in Christ alone. It is never in self-imputed suffering!

> Christ hath redeemed us from the curse of the law, being made a curse for us: for it is written, Cursed is every one that hangeth on a tree: That the blessing of Abraham might come on the Gentiles through Jesus Christ; that we might receive the promise of the Spirit through faith (Galatians 3:13-14).

I also hear this cry of desire to please God coming often from a heart who considers itself a failure, being overpowered by personal weakness. At times, I have seen this cry turn into an unholy passion to suppress guilt of prior failure.

Guilt is far too carnal an agent to give obedience to. It is far too corrupt and impure and particularly powerless. Guilt is a cry that seeks relief through outdoing the infection it created within. It wants to keep man busy. It has sent many into a mission field. Guilt is the ass that carries us along the vineyards of Balaam. The cry within—desiring to bless heaven with our life in some form—comes from guilt, and it feels repressive. It desires to please God with something that comes from our hands.

Many say they believe the promises of God, but they are not willing to act upon His Word.

My dear friend, may I suggest to you two things that produce a burst of joy in heaven and before Almighty God Himself? I have found only two specific truths that cause this jubilation in heaven: A heart turning to true repentance, and a man exercising his faith in God—these cause joy in heaven.

This is not what most desire to hear. But without question, these actions are most important in the kingdom of God.

When we find the dramatic, heart-softening wonder of true repentance from our own way and of turning our entire life toward God, surrendering the crumbs of our lives at the feet of Jesus, then there is joy in heavenly places.

Likewise, I say unto you, there is joy in the presence of the angels of God over one sinner that repenteth (Luke 15:10).

The other action by which we please Almighty God is exercising faith in His written Word. Believing the promises by faith pleases God.

> But without faith it is impossible to please him: for he that cometh to God must believe that he is, and that he is a rewarder of them that diligently seek him (Hebrews 11:6).

Many say they believe the promises of God, but they are not willing to act upon His Word. This is the sin of unbelief, and it will prevent you from entering the land of His promises.

According to the written Word, if there is anything you can do that affects the heavens, angels, and the Godhead, it is these two personal things. These two truths were constantly obvious in the teachings and life of Jesus.

Once these two truths have become your life, it is limitless what God can do with your future for His glory.

But not until then.

Could this cry for spiritual richness be to take us to the end of ourselves so that our dependence rests upon a power higher than the meager ability of man?

There was this truth in Jesus, that He could not do anything without the Father. If the holy Son of God could not, how is it that most think *they* can, and can even find personal fulfillment in it? The answer is a simple one. Jesus did only spiritual work with eternal results.

> Then answered Jesus and said unto them, Verily, verily, I say unto you, **The Son can do nothing of himself**, but what he seeth the Father do: for what things soever he doeth, these also doeth the Son likewise (John 5:19).

Oh, how solemn the depth of surrender was in the Son of God! This depth of change does not come by strategic modifications of thinking patterns in my self man. It comes alone in true dying to personal enablement and giftedness of mortal man, regardless how spiritual he might seem!

Jesus, the Son of Almighty God, did not say that He chose to do nothing outside the Father. He confessed that He could do nothing of Himself. May I repeat His confession! Jesus did not say, "I *choose* to do nothing." He confessed, "I *can* do nothing of myself."

The depth of the Father's inner working was far deeper within Jesus than mere "notion." Jesus found within Himself the inability to do anything by the power of His natural man. Within the limits of his natural thinking, the natural man will never understand this dishonoring weakness. Rather, the power of self is esteemed in the worldly Christian as personal strength; it is admirable and is even well thought of.

Can we imagine the wrestling within the heart of Jesus, still a thirty-year-old tradesman, maintaining the daily duties of trade in Nazareth, but yearning to redeem the world? Was He tempted with thoughts like we are? Yes indeed! In all points like we are!

How can I continue the work of my hands as a tradesman, while people are dying without a plan of redemption? Do I need to quit my job at once and run to do what I am called to do?

Jesus knew perfectly well that He needed something that He did not have as of yet. The Son of God needed personal empowerment from on High.

Here we see the absolute dependence that Jesus was subjected to by the internal work of the mighty hand of God. He was entirely submitted to the provisional power that comes alone by hope through faith. Yet all seemed entirely invisible as He worked with the hammer.

Now that we know the story, the working out of the plan was so absolutely observable. It was the perfect substance of faith. Jesus waited with much patience.

After the submission of baptism in the water, the Dove came and rested upon His life. Now, for the first time, we read that Jesus was Spirit-led. And where was He led? Into the mission field? Into the temple? No, no, no!

Into the wilderness, with fasting for forty days and nights. God's sovereign work within Jesus started in the boot camp of a wilderness. Jesus was led into the wilderness of horror by the Holy Spirit, and the wilderness took all the natural ability of man from Him.

But when He came out of the wilderness, He came in the power of the Holy Spirit. What did the wilderness do to the Son of God? It empowered Him to move in the Holy Spirit. It was His only survival! Satan was strong around Him with kingdom-altering temptations, but He was led by the Spirit and returned in the power of the Spirit. He came out of the wilderness as the most powerful man ever to walk the earth. And three years after He was baptized with water and with the Holy Spirit in Jordan, He cried with a loud voice from the cross, "It is finished!"

This is what a real wilderness will do. The problem with many Christians today is that we avoid the wilderness because we refuse complete surrender and consecration. The testimony of Jesus was a simple one. "I can do nothing of myself." He learned complete dependency on the power from heaven.

Jesus came in the flesh like one of us, yet He was without sin. His personal ability gave Him no confidence to do the things required to be our Savior. It was the confession of inability that brought Him to spiritual ability. Within the framework of this humility He now could learn obedience through the things He suffered. Others had seen the power that worked in Him, but now on the cross they mocked His faith. "Where is your power to deliver yourself from our nails we placed in your hands?" He endured beyond humiliation.

> He saved others; himself he cannot save. If he be the King of Israel, let him now come down from the cross, and we will believe him. He trusted in God; let him deliver him now, if he will have him: for he said, I am the Son of God (Matthew 27:42-43).

Jesus was the completely unesteemed, classic outcast in all of God's kingdom history. He was despitefully dealt with, until His deficiency became His confession. Even the Son of God can do nothing of Himself—yet before He became man, He created the world! He saw His human empowerment to be His eternal deficiency. Jesus was in the form of Almighty God yet lowered Himself by personal obedience in death, even on the cross, to the last beat of His heart.

> Who, being in the form of God, thought it not robbery to be equal with God: But made himself of no reputation, and took upon him the form of a servant, and was made in the likeness of men: And being found in fashion as a man, he humbled himself, and **became obedient unto death, even the death of the cross** (Philippians 2:6-8).

Again, Jesus did not say I can do nothing *by* myself. He confessed, "I can do nothing *of* myself".

Until I come to this confession of personal truth in knowing Him and the power of His resurrection and the fellowship of His sufferings, God will never do His mighty exploits for His glory through my life.

> But the people that do know their God shall be strong, and do exploits (Daniel 11:32).

The fellowship of His sufferings is done at the potter's house, by the power of the Spirit. This is where we learn to be bent and reshaped for usefulness to the Master. The hammer and the anvil mark us with love—precious love that drives out all fear. It is the shaping of the candlestick in Revelation.

I hereby confess that everything I do without the Father is entirely temporal. Only by way of eternal power, which originates alone from eternal God and is alone by faith, can anything eternal be done.

> All things were made by him; and without him was not anything made that was made (John 1:3).

I maintain that this verse has not changed one jot or one tittle.

Joshua and Caleb were in the wilderness for forty years, going in circles with the unbelieving children of Israel. After they stepped out of the wilderness across the Jordan River just several miles away, they destroyed Jericho, the oldest city of the day, by faith—without touching it! It was done entirely by faith.

By faith Joshua killed thirty-one kings and overthrew the same amount of cities. Because he did this in faith, they are still destroyed. The fallen walls of Jericho and the blackened fire marks of Hazor are to this day a seal that when God destroys, it will not be resurrected.

The purpose of spiritual faith is to open the door by the finger of God, so that His written Word will be fulfilled in every situation.

CHAPTER 5

Pioneers of Faith

*L*et us look at examples of the pioneers and heroes of faith. **Paul** found the same truth concerning his personal ability. Undisputedly the most prolific writer of the Holy New Testament, yet he describes his preaching presentation and ministry: "I was before you in weakness and in fear and much trembling."

> And my speech and my preaching was not with enticing words of man's wisdom, but in demonstration of the Spirit and of power (1 Corinthians 2:4).

Popular preaching stars of our day, where the numbers gather, have a presentation obstructively different. It is a glamorous event and a display of fashion and eloquence that outdates the cross. Paul said that he did not use persuasive manipulations, worldly wisdom from manuals, and scholarly concepts to entice and impress. Quite contrary to modern thinking, he truly found that his personal strength was a handicap to his spiritual ability.

Paul said, furthermore, that he was among the best in zeal, assuring his beliefs, and blameless concerning the law. This man was the best of the best! But he declared all his ambition and ability was like dung and not useful when it came to his spiritual man.

He saw that heaven's empowerment was imperative for any lasting changes within his soul. He knew that unless all his own options and abilities became as dead, God would be unable to raise anything heavenly from them.

> Yea doubtless, and I count all things but loss for the excellency of the knowledge of Christ Jesus my Lord: for whom I have suffered the **loss of all things**, and **do count them but dung**, that I may win Christ (Philippians 3:8).

The carnal man thinks himself strong, with many abilities and crafty thoughts. Paul declares that when he was weak, then alone was he strong. God's strength was made perfect in Paul's weakness. Faith emanates from this state.

How do I become perfect in weakness? I surrender the natural man to complete dependence on the higher power of invisible, Almighty God by the Holy Spirit. This is the substance of faith.

The carnal man counterbalances weakness with self-empowerment, in trying harder and harder to become what he thinks he ought to be. He will boast in his achievements and flaunt them for all to see. This can even be through subtle pride of voluntary humility and self-depravation, out of which he secretly longs to gain a remarkable reputation and competitive notability. The carnal man in the eyes of a carnal man is a great man. He will have produced many sons of personal accomplishment. One problem however: They are his own sons, not God's sons.

By far, the most remarkable fact of Paul's life was the power and demonstration that emanated from his life. His manuscript was not filled with how it should all work when one preaches or ministers. His deepest impact was the life he lived of genuine demonstration of the Holy Spirit and power! People were changed by the Holy Spirit, not as a result of extended altar calls begging and counting responses, as is popular in Christian society today. (I don't know if I have ever seen a coaxed-in saint. They are born, sometimes with great agony, desiring a desperate change that only heaven can offer.)

> One of the greatest things that man can ever discover is to see what God sees within.

This is part of the reason that the church has lost its power. We have turned away from presenting genuine repentance so that we can count numbers. Today, the church houses are filled with unrepentant sinners, and in some instances, they are even praising the Lord. But there is no remission of sins without true repentance.

> And he came into all the country about Jordan,
> preaching the baptism of repentance for the
> remission of sins (Luke 3:3).

> And that repentance and remission of sins should
> be preached in his name among all nations,
> beginning at Jerusalem (Luke 24:47).

True repentance is never a shallow experience! It is an enormously deep surrender and confession of the ill, dark, sin-festering dilemmas in the hidden self life.

If repentance is experienced correctly, it opens the heart to much deeper cleansing. Now God can reveal His further perfecting with heavenly empowerment by His truth.

> He hath stripped me of my glory, and taken the
> crown from my head (Job 19:9).

The shallow experiences often observed in contemporary services in our day yield little besides sensationalistic entertainment. The work of God is a spiritual work, with heavenly transformations that are unquestionably miraculous.

The church has become attracted to shallow "commitments" rather than holy transformations that create children of God. Birth is not a commitment! New birth is genuine and leaves no doubt to its divine operation and even causes heaven to rejoice when one soul repents.

We can no longer rejoice over one soul at the altar. Why not? Because the numbers are not big enough to make an impression! But the cry and eagerness of heaven have become apparent, and I believe, even desperate for one soul who finds true repentance.

> I say unto you, that likewise joy shall be in heaven over one sinner that repenteth, more than over ninety and nine just persons, which need no repentance (Luke 15:7).

Does this abundant joy in heaven occur because true repentance happens so seldom? I understand the glory of the return of the backslider, but it is not another commitment.

Repentance is a divine surrender of the old wasted carnal man with years of failure and spiritual demise. True and genuine evangelism is not by witty words or winning an argument. True success in ministry that lasts into eternity is by deep nights of weeping and breaking before the throne of God in continual personal surrender, regardless of the cost.

It is with fear and much trembling when we are given a moment to stand in the most precious place between God and man. We cannot waste a minute in our own ability when we stand behind the pulpit. The spiritual ministry upon our life is alone effective when we embrace the cross and walk in the glorious realm of faith. The cost of this is tremendous! It is misunderstood and ridiculed and despised by man—and rejoiced over in heaven.

Before we dare think about *numbers*, let us consider *sons*. Before we think about *leaders*, let us consider *disciples*.

Remember Abram's son Ishmael was a son to Abram. But in three different places, God called Isaac Abraham's "only" son. Did God not reckon Ishmael as Abraham's son?

> And he said, Take now thy son, **thine only son Isaac**, whom thou lovest, and get thee into the land of Moriah; and offer him there for a burnt offering upon one of the mountains which I will tell thee of (Genesis 22:2).

There are many sons of good intention. But carnal sons of good intention are not sons of God. I am speaking in spiritual terms.

I believe at the judgment seat of Christ, all sons, including myself, will be examined of what sort they are. Not what size or how many sons there are, but of what sort they are.

> Every man's work shall be made manifest: for the day shall declare it, because it shall be revealed by fire; and the fire shall try every man's work of what sort it is (1 Corinthians 3:13).

The judgment of Christ will be a fire. It will burn everything that can burn. The only deeds that will not burn are those that have the seal of God's work of fire. Gold, silver, and precious stones are the only products that were spiritual, and the fire could not consume them, because the fire had purified them long before.

According to Revelation 13:18, and many Bible scholars, the number "six" is the number of man. We notice that the six qualities of man's work were all built upon the eternal foundation which was Jesus Christ. Three were purified in the fire, while three were destroyed in the fire. Herein lies the vast difference between the spiritual man's faith and the carnal man's work.

Notice the three all capable of coming about through natural growth: wood from a tree; hay from a plant; and stubble from wheat. Things can be quickly built with wood, hay, and stubble, and such structures can appear large and effective.

When you look at the structure that has been built with gold, silver, and precious stones, there is a huge difference in size. The only building that can be done with gold and silver is done so by purifying and shaping. Precious stones cannot be grown; only when the bench jeweler works the precision cuts does the stone reveal its preciousness.

One sort of work is large and visible and impressive to the natural man. The other work seems small and insignificant. The carnal man looks at size, which impresses the multitudes and is a great fundraiser to display. The spiritual man looks at eternal value and offers little to impress the eyes of natural man.

The fire comes by way of the Holy Spirit and the cross; the two can never be separated.

If fire can destroy everything that I am and have, I must know that I am nothing already. Hereby, we can know what we are—and whether the fire is welcome today or not.

✧

Do I have weakness? Do I understand weakness?

I have much weakness, and to admit weakness is humbling to the proud, self-made man.

One of the greatest things that man can ever discover is to see what God sees within. He sees man's weakness.

The carnal man considers personal weakness as defeat. God sees it as precious. Jesus says He uses weakness to make strength perfect.

The natural man calls weakness uselessness and seems embarrassed and defeated by it. God calls weakness usefulness and sees working material to then produce from His perfection.

God uses our weakness and His spiritual strength permeates through it. Our own strength is much too monstrous and boastful for God to use.

> And he said unto me, My grace is sufficient for thee: for my strength is made perfect in weakness. Most gladly therefore will I rather glory in my infirmities, that the power of Christ may rest upon me (2 Corinthians 12:9).

I don't think I have to write about what weakness is. If people can be transparent and honest, most are well aware of what they consider their own spiritual weakness.

Most are not aware that God can only and truly work through weakness to make His strength secure. A man is brought to true dependence on God and the Holy Spirit once weakness is surrendered. God's resurrecting power overcomes our weakness if we allow it to be so by faith.

Grace is the supernatural power that comes upon a man's honest, non-embarrassed surrender when he experiences deep contrition through faith in Jesus Christ. Grace hovers like a cloud of power over the poor soul who has now, in the presence of God, become honest and real concerning his weakness. This is the marvelous endowing power from the mercy of God to man's surrendered disability!

Grace is one of the most misunderstood words in the Bible. Grace is divine, enabling power, not heavenly license or glorious leniency.

> For by grace are ye saved through faith; and that not of yourselves: it is the gift of God (Ephesians 2:8).

For by divine influence, the enabling power of heaven, are we saved through faith, not from ourselves. It is God's gift!

Joseph was the first son of Jacob and Rachel. Rachel could not have children until God gave her the miracle of her life and Joseph was born. How wonderful was Joseph's beginning—a total miracle that the finger of God had to touch the womb of Rachel so that she could conceive. He was a unique child, as his coat of many colors indicated. All who saw him saw someone special, someone different than most.

Checking on the well-being of his elder brothers in the Shechem valley was a path Joseph blazed in obedience to his father and in seeming innocence. These were prophetic footprints of his future, as God started the process of making Joseph one of His men.

His brothers deemed him worthless and worthy of death, and he was thrown into a dry well. This well could easily have been dug by Abram years earlier when he landed in the valley of Shechem.

Next Joseph was stripped of the royal coat and sold to the enemy. His hard-working brothers saw no royalty in this God-favored seventeen-year-old.

> He hath stripped me of my glory, and taken the crown from my head (Job 19:9).

At the young age of seventeen, Joseph was being prepared by God for a spiritual job ahead. His coat of royalty was ripped apart, and Joseph was in a pit of unknown destiny. Freedom from the confinement of a waterless well would come only in his sale as a slave to idolatrous Egypt.

Now Joseph belonged to the Ishmaelites and was on his way to slavery. He was sold again when he was bought to work as a housekeeper in the home of a chief captain of Pharaoh. After he fled the temptation of Potiphar's wife, he was thrown into a prison.

Joseph was in that dungeon for several years. In the eyes of common man, this young lad was as God-forsaken as a man could imagine. He was mistreated, misunderstood, despised, falsely accused, and imprisoned in a dungeon of horror. How can someone seem more God-forsaken? What in the world had this poor lad done to come under so much abuse?

God was preparing Joseph for His use!

Let us take a quick scan of the life of Joseph up to this point. He meant well in obeying his father and searching for his brothers. Then thrown into a dry well. Sold to the Ishmaelites and given a cruel free ride into Egypt (exactly where God wanted him). Sold again to work in a chief military captain's house. Fled from the temptation of fornication with the wife of Potiphar. Lost his coat again! Sentenced to sit in a dark prison cell for several years. Made to look like a mad man.

How could Joseph not be bitter and angry with God for the misuse and terrible false accusations? The answer is clear: He had a dream about his calling and held faith that God was in complete control to take him and make him and place him, regardless of the cost.

Joseph's experience in exile was God's spiritual training camp. I do not know that we fully understand the inner workings and the awfulness of what Joseph endured. God had to make this boy into a man, a man of His own. He made Joseph a man of faith to work the work of God. God had to remove all self-man, identity, ability, prominence, favor, and honor from Joseph, and He did this by way of misrepresentation through false accusations and misunderstandings. This was done so that Joseph could be one of God's men.

Joseph lost his coat of identity twice. Both losses resulted from the evil deeds of the enemy. True men of God will lose their coats more than once. The last coat that is placed upon God's men cannot be removed by man, because it is not visible to man.

Egypt was the oldest, most powerful country in the world. It was an evil world empire of idolatry and the center of worship of many false gods. The subject is much too complex to write about in short form, but I have been to Egypt, and I've seen firsthand the forms of evil idolatry that are still highly visible among the many temples Egypt built to its gods. This dynasty of idolatry is ultimately what God wanted to bring to its knees before He could bring the promises of Israel's habitation to fulfillment. So God placed a young man next to Pharaoh and kept him there till it was the appointed time.

When Joseph revealed his identity to his betraying brothers, this is what he said about the incident that had happened many years earlier:

> Now therefore be not grieved, nor angry with yourselves, that ye sold me hither: **for God did send me before you to preserve life** (Genesis 45:5).

> But as for you, ye thought evil against me; but God meant it unto good, to bring to pass, as it is this day, to save much people alive (Genesis 50:20).

Joseph was not bitter. There was no complaining. No throwing in the towel in discouragement. He knew by faith that God would never take him where he was not meant to be. Whether in a pit, sold to the enemy, in a captain's house, in a prison, or sitting in the seat of the second highest in the land, he was where God had led him.

He was in the presence of Almighty God! This was the environment he lived in. Faith in God's provision, regardless of surroundings and what life seems to offer, is where God wants His man to trust and not be dismayed, even when he is misunderstood and misrepresented. The true man of God lives in the presence of God, regardless what coat of identity is taken from him or how he may be presented.

Moses, a Hebrew baby floating among the bulrushes, hidden because of death threats, was found and placed among the finest palaces of the pharaoh in Egypt. He was an unusual child at the palace—a Hebrew from the gentle ripples of the great Nile and hand-placed by God.

Moses grew up as a well-educated man, taught by the esteemed educators of the day. He was a mighty speaker, and his words reflected his wisdom, abilities, and power.

> And Moses was learned in all the wisdom of the Egyptians, and was **mighty in words** and in deeds (Acts 7:22).

As an adopted kin to the pharaoh, Moses would also have had proper honor, respect, and personal dignity instilled within his character.

Egypt stood as the symbol of pomp, power, and riches—far beyond any country of that day, even more so than Babylon. I am still astonished at the stunning ability that made possible the building of temples and structures Egypt constructed thousands of years ago. The powers they possessed were attributed to the gods they worshipped.

This idolatry originated with the descendants of Noah's son Ham. He was the rebel of Noah's three sons. Ham's lineage traces links to Cush, to Nimrod, and then to Mizraim, which is the Hebrew word for Egypt.

The generational fallout in occultism spread quickly through the generations of Ham, and it appears that Nimrod and his wife invented post-flood astrology. Nimrod most likely conceived and established the original twelve zodiac constellations, including Sagittarius, the archer, probably named after himself, the mighty hunter. (The correct interpretation of *hunter* is *fighter*.) Cain and his lineage were mighty fighters—still apparent in the Mideast conflict to this day.

According to secular history, Nimrod intertwined astrology with astronomy, a system which was followed and esteemed until the sixteenth century's scientific renaissance in Europe.

In the evil empire of Egypt, this vehement idolatry invented worship of the "mother goddess," the sun god Ra, Osiris, god of the underworld, and many more.

Moses would also have been well educated in the crafts of this idolatry of Egypt. But Moses was a Hebrew with the promises of the God of Abraham, Isaac, and Jacob in his heart. He inventoried all the benefits he had experienced being brought up as a prince, and he decided there was greater purpose in being a servant of Almighty God.

At the age of forty, Moses was moved to visit the land of his Hebrew brethren, in the plains of Goshen, Egypt. His heart was obviously grieved when he saw their slavery and cruel mistreatment. At one point, he struck an Egyptian to death after the Egyptian had treated one of the Hebrew men with brutality. Moses felt the burden of justice upon himself and rectified the wrong by the hand of his own physical power.

The calling of Moses was obvious, but it was not yet made a spiritual calling. He was still a well-educated self-man, immersed in royalty. Yet he was missing the deep power of personal brokenness. His complete dependence and faith had to be divinely placed in a higher power before God would step into His resident lordship.

Moses needed to have his calling made a spiritual calling, and there is one alone who can do it.

> By faith Moses, when he was come to years, refused to be called the son of Pharaoh's daughter; Choosing rather to suffer affliction with the people of God, than to enjoy the pleasures of sin for a season; Esteeming the reproach of Christ greater riches than the treasures in Egypt: for he had respect unto the recompence of the reward. By faith he forsook Egypt, not fearing the wrath of the king: for he endured, as **seeing him who is invisible** (Hebrews 11:24-27).

Moses ran for his life and escaped into the deserts of Arabia, remaining there for forty years as a man of personal failure before God. Forty years of learning at the highest levels of the land was useless in a desert where prominence was as dust and loneliness was his kin. Moses knew the palace life, but God wanted him to learn desert life.

> He hath stripped me of my glory, and taken the crown from my head (Job 19:9).

Moses was undone for forty years in the desert, until he knew and remembered little from his past and his future was naught. I am sure Moses had to give up his burden to save his brethren who were in slavery. And then—and only then—did Holy God El-Shaddai become everything in His life.

God has to dry up our dreams, wishes, and desires, regardless how important they might seem. You will never become spiritual until all has died and vanished, like Abraham's Isaac on the altar of surrender on Moriah. What Moses thought was his "calling" lay in shattered dreams, mingled with tears, until even tears were a stranger in his wilderness of defeat. The calling lay helpless in surrender in the dusty desert of the Arabian sands. The tears had long evaporated, and the dream of a lifetime had disintegrated and was perhaps only vaguely remembered.

Let us take a careful note, this calling became resident in Moses when he first saw the slavery of his own brethren.

Forty years later—in a moment—all changed when Moses saw the picture as God had seen it all along. Among God's first words after the forty years was the line, "I also saw the afflictions of your brethren." God had been silent for forty years, but now seemed to be saying that what Moses had seen back there, God had seen as well.

The problem here is that Moses had not been through his personal school of leadership yet. Moses had to first wander aimlessly for forty long years.

Forty years later, after all was dried up, God spoke and confirmed the calling as Moses declared he was unable to speak and thus became qualified and ended up becoming one of the greatest of all Old Testament patriarchs.

He saw that his life was like a burning bush that wasted away no further. It was a fire, an unusual fire that was burning, and a heavenly angel was speaking out of it.

Now God called Moses from that desert of loneliness, trials, and despair and said, "Take off those shoes, Moses! You have been walking on holy ground. I have been with you all along and have watched and have personally been making you for myself."

This is the true making of a man of God! That day, Moses was shown that what seemed to be a hiding place, forsaken of all hope of ever being used by God again, was a holy place.

The Sinai wilderness was the place for making a natural man into a spiritual man. This heavenly school of Horeb was not conditioned with human grandeur. It was the place of forty years of unlearning, so that Moses could know the power of God.

Only at the end of this holy unlearning wilderness time could God introduce Himself as the great I AM THAT I AM. The bush was so far deteriorated from its own strength that the burning fire could not consume its branches. The bush did not burn away.

When the self man has been through the fire of God so deeply, the fire of the Holy Spirit burns by His own power upon the man. Herein is where the fire of God sustains itself as it burns for the glory of God.

The fiery angel upon the bush told Moses to go back to Egypt. When Moses heard this, He made this statement:

> And Moses said unto the LORD, O my Lord, **I am not eloquent**, neither heretofore, nor since thou hast spoken unto thy servant: but **I am slow of speech, and of a slow tongue** (Exodus 4:10).

Let us consider again that New Testament verse:

> And Moses was learned in all the wisdom of the Egyptians, and was mighty in words and in deeds (Acts 7:22).

What had changed?

Moses, with a fast and well-qualified tongue and elevated ability, was disqualified from the palace of Pharaoh in order to make him a mouthpiece for God. Now, Moses' slow and disabled tongue from the desert wilderness of Jabal al-Lawz made him a God-qualified prophet and, at the age of eighty years, the greatest leader ever.

Oh, there is nothing like being changed by the power of God through the wilderness of great loss of vision! It is here that much patience, loneliness, despair, and forsakenness by man become an acquaintance of the man of God.

What Moses thought was an escape for him in his failure ended up being a lonesome desert that changed him ever so deeply. What man observes in the deep wilderness of weeping and despair can be a place of spiritual splendor and heavenly grandeur—if you walk by faith in Almighty God!

Let us look yet at the conclusion of Israel leaving Egypt and the severe consequences that followed.

Under the power of God, from desert dust came forth the greatest leader of all time. Moses now had the proper training in his heart. He was well trained in desert sustenance by faith in the invisible God Jehovah Jireh. Moses was now to be the leader of several million people who were under heavy slave mentality in a foreign land. These Hebrews were the sons of Israel. God needed a spiritual man to lead Israel through years of spiritual and environmental extremities.

It was a task that would have extreme challenges in the modern day, from an environmental point of view alone. The desert was desolate, hot, scant of water and food, torturous, and disorienting. The children of Israel were locked into this environment for forty

When the self man has been through the fire of God so deeply, the fire of the Holy Spirit burns by His own power upon the man.

years to teach them to believe every word that proceeded from the mouth of God.

> And he humbled thee, and suffered thee to hunger, and fed thee with manna, which thou knewest not, neither did thy fathers know; **that he might make thee know** that man doth not live by bread only, **but by every word that proceedeth out of the mouth of the LORD doth man live** (Deuteronomy 8:3).

God intends to do what we can't so that He alone can do it completely and correctly and the glory is all His. To do His work by His power alone, He has to diminish His kingdom child to personal weakness.

At the most critical part of the Israelites' journey to escape the terror of Egypt, God needed the humble wooden rod of Moses. He had brought the millions in sandals to the Red Sea—and now they were trapped, with no way to escape. The most elite, battle-proven Egyptian military, "the best in the world," with Pharaoh and his sons and the best captains, were right behind them. Now what?

The Israelites stood there without a path or bridge to cross over. Moses was their leader, and he looked like a complete failure.

The children of Israel had two impossible options. They could climb the mountains of Nuweiba right behind them, which are an extreme and abrupt vertical challenge—impossible to climb. (I have seen this with my own eyes.) Or they could take option number two, and drown in the Red Sea right in front of them.

I repeat, faith comes forth where a spiritual man's weakness abounds. It is in the transpiring of this truth where God's finger moves with His mighty miracles. When you see a miracle, this is what has happened.

Moses placed the rod ("the rod of transition," Hebrew) of God upon the water, and the wind started to blow!

Let us consider the rod for a moment. This was the rod that knew Moses and witnessed the extreme trial in the wilderness forty years. It had all the personal history of Moses within it. It was the echo of sounds too deep to understand at Horeb, when Moses had lost all he had. This was the rod that had turned into a snake when Moses threw it down. God asked Moses to take it up by the tail, and it became known as the rod of God.

Here is the same principle again. The tail is all that we may have, and herein it becomes the rod of God! Oh how glorious is this revelatory truth!

The promised provision was all given when Moses saw the bush on fire. God said, "I AM THAT I AM. I AM the divider of the Red Sea—that is what I AM!"

What happened at that gigantic moment in history was the climactic purpose of why the Israel of Jacob had been in Egypt all along, sustained by the provision of Joseph. At that moment, the strong, proud, idolatrous nation of Egypt was brought to its knees!

Israel, the work force of Egypt's slave system, trained to be the greatest craftsmen of their day, was gone, carrying with them the gold and silver and all the wealth of the land. Israel was now free from the land of Egypt for the first time in over 400 years. Then at the Red Sea, the severe death blow sounded throughout the entire world that Pharaoh, his sons, the best captains, and the whole military were dead! The throne of this royal dynasty was completely devastated and abolished. The sons of the pharaoh's dynasty were all dead. The thousand-year chain of command was shattered.

History makes it clear that Egypt attributed their victories in war and all of their other successes to the gods they worshiped. They had a god for everything: the rain god, sun god, fertility god, and over a thousand other false gods they worshipped with great pomp and pride.

So which of all these gods they trusted had allowed this great defeat?

This was the devastating question for all of Egypt and its allies, a large area of territorial dominion. All their theories and philosophies were reduced to nothing in a moment! Now they realized that Israel's God was far more powerful than any god they thought they had. They realized their occultist belief system was entirely bankrupt.

The history of Egypt is of interest to me, and when you study it, you will conclude that Egypt has never recovered from that moral and spiritual blow in the Red Sea.

The human mind can never comprehend entirely the massive satanic landslide that took place that day. What was the key to the whole picture of this major victory? Moses, now a spiritual man made in the wilderness, had nothing more than a wooden rod, surrendered as the rod of God.

The rod he carried into the desert of escape was like a snake that bit his Egyptian enemy. Now it became a spiritual tool that Moses held by its tail, "the rod of God"! He placed it by faith upon the deadly waters of destruction.

Out of the same glorious separation of water that brought the Israel of God to safety came a gigantic incident that exploded and destroyed the massive influence of Egyptian occultism, as the highest in power and pageantry!

This event was the foretaste and glorious paradigm of the glory that the death and resurrection of Jesus Christ would fulfill against the power of Lucifer. Through the power of the Holy Spirit, Christ triumphantly prevailed over death and hell and Lucifer and every devil and made an open show of them for all eternity to see.

> And having spoiled principalities and powers, he made a shew of them openly, triumphing over them in it (Colossians 2:15).

What God did in Egypt, He finalized at the cross as Christ declared, "It is finished!"

Gideon came out of his hiding place, a grotto winepress, to thresh wheat in what seemed to be a wrong and dangerous place. An angel of God stood by an oak tree, bringing a message for this man who lived in grim days.

After forty years of peace brought by Deborah's victory in Canaan, she had died, and the Israelites again did evil in the sight of the Lord by worshipping other gods. This opened the door for attacks by the enemy, the Midianites and Amalekites.

When the Israelites planted their fields and vineyards, the Midianites, who lived in the Gilead mountain range, came in and stole the crops. Israel became greatly impoverished and was under continual defeat. They were driven into hiding in dens and caves in the mountains.

Into this grim situation came an angel of God to deliver a message to a man named Gideon from the least tribe of Manasseh. Gideon was threshing wheat at the winepress.

When you look at the basic differences and the purposes of the threshing floor and the winepress, it becomes apparent that Gideon was seemingly in the wrong place to be doing what he was doing. Threshing wheat was a dangerous attraction for the Midianite marauders. Why was Gideon "threshing within" at a winepress? He was desperate. They needed food. Gideon was doing the best he could with what option he had to sustain himself and those for whom he was responsible.

Those of us who have stood on the hills of the threshing floors in Israel understand why the windy location was strategic to blowing away the chaff as wheat stalks were tossed into the air. However, in the caves of the winepress, the required movement of wind was virtually nothing. Winepresses are typically not placed where there is much wind. The separating of the chaff from the wheat and the pressing of the grapes at a winepress are completely different processes.

It seems that God was doing a purifying work in Gideon, separating the wheat from chaff in Gideon's life at that time. God was making him a spiritual man in preparation for what was about to happen. While this spiritual process was taking place, Gideon ran into hiding at a winepress because of impending danger.

When you avoid the wind of God, the separating of the chaff becomes very difficult. Polite obedience severs no chaff. Threshing in the wind does.

As God separates the chaff from our life, it is embarrassing and it brings one to deep humility. It is a fearful thing! We want to run into hiding because the threshing floor experience is misunderstood by us as well as others. It is unbearable to my natural man. This is also part of God's way. Deep, humbling misunderstandings in acceptance of God's ways are often required for separation of chaff from our flesh man. And this happens right in the very eyes of the carnal man, who walks in the flesh and flaunts his blind remedies of reason as decent, common-sense solutions.

> Faith comes forth where a spiritual man's weakness abounds.

After people receive the fullness of the Holy Spirit, they are divinely placed into the hands of the divine thresher in a way that is much different than before. According to a phrase in Matthew chapter 3, we see that this is the place where God brings His child into His divine possession in all phases of life. He gathers "His wheat into the garner [meaning barn]."

> I indeed baptize you with water unto repentance: but he that cometh after me is mightier than I, whose shoes I am not worthy to bear: he shall baptize you with the Holy Ghost, and with fire: Whose fan is in his hand, and he will thoroughly purge his floor, and gather his wheat into the garner; but he will burn up the chaff with unquenchable fire (Matthew 3:11-12).

There are many professors of faith who have never surrendered their entire soul, body, and spirit to Christ, for fear they will lose what they are and have. Many easily quote that "God made Jesus Lord," which is true. But have I made Him Lord over my life? Jesus becomes Lord over my life only after I have surrendered to His lordship in *all* things.

To present oneself as a true, living sacrifice to God is a scriptural requirement. Until this is experienced, there will not be true spiritual usefulness in the kingdom of God.

Grapes and wheat are not harvested in the same time frame. So Gideon was alone and not understanding what was happening around him. Being tested by God can often cause misunderstandings concerning God and His ways.

Gideon might have questioned the hand of God, saying, "Where are the miracles that our fathers talked about? Were we not once delivered from Egypt by the Lord and are now forsaken by Him? The Midianites have robbed us seven years in a row and leave us destitute."

Gideon thought that God had forsaken Israel because they fell into the hands of the Midianites over and over again. Unless man places total trust in God, he can get greatly disoriented.

What I find remarkable, as I have walked before God for many years, is that God will turn your face before He turns your feet.

Toward what was Gideon's face turned? He had his attention on God's mission to Israel. This was his concern, and the wrestling within him continued as he wondered how he fit into this picture.

Why was this burden so heavily upon his attention? The answer is simple. There was a call upon the heart of Gideon, and God had turned Gideon's face right toward it.

As God prepared Gideon for this great commission, Gideon became perplexed with what was happening within him. He was misunderstanding, because his ability was nothing and his stature was of no prominence.

"A man like me could never be used to demonstrate God's purpose through restoration of Israel. After all, I am only of the tribe of Manasseh." The tribe of Manasseh was of no reputation because they were descendants of one of Joseph's two sons from his marriage to the Egyptian woman, a union which was forbidden by Hebrew law.

> And the Lord looked upon him, and said, Go in this thy might, and thou shalt save Israel from the hand of the Midianites: have not I sent thee? And he said unto him, Oh my Lord, wherewith shall I save Israel? behold, **my family is poor in Manasseh**, and **I am the least** in my father's house (Judges 6:14-15).

God qualified Gideon perfectly because he was weak and unqualified in his own eyes and in the eyes of man.

Faith comes forth when a spiritual man's weakness abounds. The task ahead was far too big for this man of God to be hiding among the grape hulls. Gideon seemingly saw himself as weak and fearful, yet God saw him as a strong man of might and valor. God saw his spiritual man. Gideon saw his natural man.

The preparation of the heart of Gideon was far more important than the burden he had for Israel. He could have taken the burden into his own hands and become a complete failure. Rather than that, he seemingly became a failure before God sent him into his spiritual mission.

I could continue to use numerous examples of the works of this great kingdom child, but will only use one more as I conclude.

What God did to Gideon in diminishing him, He did to the army that served under Gideon. An apparently strong 30,000 men were reduced to 300 men—and the Midianites were defeated completely to this day, through weapons of lamps, trumpets, and the voices of God and Gideon.

God had to reduce the ability of the army of Gideon because they were too high in number and too powerful and well-qualified for God. They could have dealt with the Midianites at hand without God, perhaps. But if I take things into my own hands, I take them out of God's hand. If I take things out of God's hand, then I stand alone and limited. When I stand alone and limited, I become strong in myself and vulnerable to fall. It is the natural man who wants to conquer the task by the strength of man.

God did not want the Israelite army to fight with swords—which appears to man as the only way to prevail. The carnal man has much fight within. The spiritual man has much God within.

Gideon divided the 300 into three groups of 100 and told them to do what he did at the specified time.

They gathered around the Midianite army encampment in the night while all were sleeping, even the watchmen. The three companies blew the trumpets, then broke the vessels and lifted their lights in their left hands and cried with one voice, "The sword of the Lord and of Gideon!" They continued to blow the trumpets and hold their lamps. The hosts of the enemy military were so frightened they all took their swords and started to run, and they were so confused they killed each other and fell on their own swords in sheer fright.

God easily prevailed over the dangerous Midianites. As the number of Midianites were diminished by their own swords, the other Israeli countrymen joined in the chase until the enemies were all dead or driven back to their land.

Of the people that Gideon's countrymen slew in the whole operation, only two are named in the record. Prince Oreb was slain upon a rock "threshing floor," and Prince Zeeb died by a winepress. Their heads were brought back to Gideon. One prince died where Gideon was hiding, and the other died where Gideon should have been threshing.

In the studies of God's Word, I have gleaned many things of God's revealed truth concerning faith. I have drawn conclusions from the life of Abraham, Isaac, Jacob, Joseph, Moses, Joshua, Deborah, Gideon, Elijah, Elisha, Peter, Paul, and many of God's spiritual servants of faith in the Old and the New Testament.

God has revealed His glory where these great men and women were weak and saturated with inability in the face of impossibility. The greater the impossibility of man's ability, the greater the probability of God's ability. So where man's impossibility prevails, God's probability avails.

When man dares to have faith in God whom they do not see, they will see God in ways that otherwise cannot be!

Man becomes weary and saddened when impossible spiritual obstacles arise before him. The purpose is often to dwindle the natural/self man to his dying grave in silence so that the Holy Spirit can bring him into spiritual ascension.

Spiritual ascension is finding our way to be led by the Spirit of God. This is the divine way of true sonship.

> For as many as are led by the Spirit of God, they
> are the sons of God (Romans 8:14).

Is this not where God wants His glory to be revealed? Can God be glorified with no faith, little faith, or simple faith?

> And whatsoever ye shall ask in my name, that will
> I do, that the **Father may be glorified in the Son.** If
> ye shall ask any thing in my name, I will do it. If ye
> love me, keep my commandments (John 14:13-15).

My understanding of true faith is that it is simple faith. Simple faith is often faith in understanding the significance of God's Word in relation to our inner spiritual lives. God will allow us to endure many things and to enjoy many things. Both need the same faith. The man of faith will not pick or choose.

Nothing of God's truth is outdated for the man of faith, and all is to be received for God's glory to be revealed. Not a jot or tittle will ever pass away or become outdated or obsolete. If the Word is obsolete or outdated to my thinking, then I must understand that it is I who must be updated in the Word.

I want to close this chapter with a brief narrative about the kingdom of God. Multitudes make a profession of Christianity but are obviously not part of the kingdom of God, because few go in thereat.

Consider these two verses and notice the difference between them.

> Jesus answered and said unto him, Verily, verily, I say unto thee, Except a man be born again, **he cannot see the kingdom of God** (John 3:3).

> Jesus answered, Verily, verily, I say unto thee, Except a man be born of water and of the Spirit, he cannot enter into the kingdom of God (John 3:5).

According to what Jesus says, seeing the kingdom of God and entering the kingdom of God are not the same thing. The kingdom of God is not a church or congregation of people gathering together and singing and preaching on a certain day of the week. The kingdom of God is not anything visible to the eye of man.

> And when he was demanded of the Pharisees, when the kingdom of God should come, he answered them and said, **The kingdom of God cometh not with observation**: Neither shall they say, Lo here! or, lo there! for, behold, the **kingdom of God is within you** (Luke 17:20-21).

Where then is the kingdom of God? The kingdom of God is within, and it is within those who are of a poor spirit.

> Blessed are the **poor in spirit**: for theirs is the kingdom of heaven (Matthew 5:3).

I want to make this perfectly clear. The "poor in spirit" are not those who misinterpret the Bible or make inconvenient verses obsolete. The poor in spirit are not some reckless, misunderstanding souls who are calloused in opinions. The poor in spirit are neither innocents nor those who are neglectful.

The poor in spirit are those who have poverty of heart and spirit because of God's deep hand upon their lives. They are those who have been tried through much tribulation for God's sake alone.

Many go through tribulation and trials—but not for God's sake. Suffering for the sake of righteousness is one thing. Suffering for mistakes and erroneous decisions and actions is entirely different, and the results are vastly different.

Suffering for the sake of righteousness is about going through tribulations and trials that come because of loving God, and this suffering often has to do with deep rejection. There is almost nothing that can break a man as deeply as rejection because of his godly life.

Notice the life of Jesus. His example shows us that suffering in rejection surrenders the heart of man to the Master of love and understanding and separates us unto Almighty God. I know much about this, having experienced this rejection throughout most of my life.

Spiritual rejection of God's men comes from carnal man, as rejection came between Cain and Abel, Jacob and Esau, and at the very end, will come between the bride and the harlot. But there is a spiritual purpose in it. It causes deep contrition, brokenness, and humbling of the heart and aids in the making of a spiritual man. So far in my life, God has seen it necessary for me to walk this way. My only option is to endure in His wonderful grace.

> Confirming the souls of the disciples, and exhorting them to continue in the faith, and that we must **through much tribulation enter into the kingdom of God** (Acts 14:22).

We see also from Jesus' words that the kingdom of God can only enter someone who can receive it as a little child.

> Verily I say unto you, Whosoever shall not receive the kingdom of God as a little child, he shall not enter therein (Mark 10:15).

To become as a little child is not an easy thing. The proud man has to have his self man defeated and broken by the power of the cross, a breaking much deeper than man can achieve himself. The carnal man is brutish when his life is challenged and he has no alternatives but to surrender. He moves into a mode of self-pity when he runs out of answers and becomes humiliated.

In making a spiritual man, God will take him to places where there are seasons of no answers. These are places that take us up the Calvary road of loneliness and the unknown. Here we find the One who has led us in a personal way. Here the Father's hand reunites us with His wooing love and understanding. Here we start to see the picture and it causes us to collapse like a little child.

This is the place of losing the self life for Christ, and until I do, I will not find my life.

> He that findeth his life shall lose it: and he that loseth his life for my sake shall **find it** (Matthew 10:39).

The mighty and rich man is filled with many answers and quick solutions from Egypt. While we might not have the answer as easily, there is a difference in us—the power embedded within by the pleading of the Holy Spirit.

We have to be brought to the one answer alone: It is no more about "I." Self has to be broken down from its abilities and challenged with things that bring us to a poor and contrite spirit, so that we can receive the Word with trembling.

For this to happen, there is much tribulation, rejection, distress—and deep sovereign moments with Almighty God! If the rich self man does not pass this test but remains in charge, too proud to go down as a child, he will not enter the kingdom because he is too large for the hole in the needle and cannot enter.

Until man has the kingdom of God within, he will not be of much value in the work of Almighty God in this world but will fall into the category of unbelief.

The kingdom of God is not in what we say, it is in power and demonstration of the Spirit.

> For the kingdom of God is not in word, but in power (1 Corinthians 4:20).

The Lord diminishes His man so far that he has only one thing to lean on. A stick is all he needs. It is where big becomes little and little becomes big! Then the sea opens, the lame are healed, the deaf hear, the enemy is made to run, the mouth of Baal is stopped, deserts are turned into fields and fields turned into harvest, and the harvest is great but the laborers of these fields are few.

There is much joy and peace where the power of God finds rest.

> For the kingdom of God is not meat and drink; but righteousness, and peace, and joy in the Holy Ghost (Romans 14:17).

This is where God's men walk by faith before God, doing the works of God, and God is greatly glorified!

CHAPTER 6

Protocol of Faith

My life has been revolutionized and transformed by the divine power of the Holy Spirit and His overflowing wisdom. Men of great faith have left a deep impact on my life and changed my realm of influence in spiritual endeavors concerning God's promises to those who believe.

I want to bring an understanding of the limitless attributes found in simple faith. I want to unfold the truth that caused the Son of God to declare His profound marvel at a truth He had never seen displayed before in all of Israel. The complexity yet simplicity of this rare statement concerns an astounding success that few of God's people have understood and experienced.

So that you can appreciate what the Holy Spirit has taught me about the faith I believe in, I also want to share my understanding of faith, based on the experiences of my life.

My landscape of experience comes from living over sixty years and from dealing with problems in thousands of people's lives through my ministry of more than thirty years. If I could write about every experience in helping and bringing deliverance to people, I could write many books. Having traveled in every state, most Canadian provinces, and twenty-four countries, I'm familiar with many diversities of place and culture.

I have seen the mighty work of God and the strength of man's work without God. This has provided a balance of perception that has helped me understand in dimensions few have had the privilege of experiencing.

For the first time in my life, I want to give you a bit of insight into my life and present specific achievements and successes. I do this to make a point that I deem necessary concerning the subject of faith.

My educational background is a simple one that 99 percent of all people could achieve. I have a ninth-grade education. I failed the fifth grade, with over 27 *F* grades on my test scores in that year alone. I was close to a straight-*D* student and remember having had only several *A* grades in my entire school experience.

My future lay before me as a victim of small intelligence. This was confirmed by my classmates as well as my father, who declared me hopeless and incapacitated concerning learning abilities and future achievements. I was not just scorned as stupid, but was considered outright asinine. I was vapid and ignorant.

I give you a picture of who I am now for the sole purpose of making a statement that I truly believe is the secret to spiritual success in active perseverance by simple faith toward God.

Here are a few specifics: I've had the privilege of saving a drowning man (which might make me a hero). I serve as an advisor, a counselor, a personal coach, a director, an analyst, an orator, the founder of multiple companies, an entrepreneur, and an employer of many wonderful people. Few people know that I am the sole owner of all the companies I own. I am also an author, a writer, a pastor, and a church founder. The ministry God has called me into has been self-supporting for over thirty years. I'm a radio preacher, a pilot, a heavy equipment operator, a land developer, a designer, an artist, an active musician, and even an advanced certified barista. I am a professional photographer and cinematographer. I hold copyrights.

I acknowledge being a lover of life and duty. In all my successes, I have never received any civic awards or trophies. I choose to not be visible.

My inner feelings are those of an underachiever. My confidence level is based alone in the God I know and the faith He introduced me to. God saw me as a trepid man with dejected emotions in the debris of shredded failure. He chose me to glorify Him with the richness of nothing.

My intention in this is to cause you to gain respect for and confidence in God's powerful Word, which is filled with promises of provision experienced through simple faith.

God did not author His holy book to be tossed as a Frisbee into the winds of the unknown. This book called the Bible is written to bring both visible and invisible glory to the master architectural Designer. The wisdom in this holy book is "the Word" of God's plan for and acceptance of mankind.

His book is not a personal manual. It is spiritual, and unless we receive it in this way, it becomes optional for man to live by it. This unique book is not a book of information to satisfy the inquisitive intellectual mind with quips or astute notions. Its power is not to create personal greatness. This holy book is marked with, "Use for eternal purpose only." It is the book of life! This book is so eternal that heaven and earth will not outlive it. It will never lose strength, and no jot or tittle will vanish from its content.

The ineffectiveness of the Bible's content occurs when a condition called faith is missing in the understanding and reading of it. How can the same Word that framed the heavens and the earth become dormant among those for whom it was intended? The ability and strength of God in and through His Word is far greater and stronger than any man can ever formulate.

This will raise the question, why then does it not work a far greater power within?

> That Christ may dwell in your hearts by faith; that ye, being rooted and grounded in love, May be able to comprehend, with all saints, what is the breadth, and length, and depth, and height, And to know the love of Christ, which passeth knowledge, that ye might be filled with all the fullness of God (Ephesians 3:17-19).

That we might know Christ's love that is beyond knowledge and that we might be *filled with all the fullness of God!*

How filled are we with God's fullness? This is a question of great concern and determines whether we are in faith or unbelief! The unbelieving fall into a group that is among the worst of sinners, according to Revelation 21:8, and will receive a more severe judgment than most would willingly acknowledge. How will we escape if we neglect so great a salvation?

Let us not be baffled with the next verse. This should burst a flood of deep contrition over our soul and cause us to seek an end to our weakness and casualness of heart.

> Now unto him that is able to do exceeding abundantly above all that we ask or think, according to the power that worketh in us (Ephesians 3:20).

For God to do exceedingly above our thinking and asking, there is a condition that needs to be met. He can only do that which worketh in us already. This is where the intrinsic value of many professing Christians falls far short of the glory of God.

It is necessary to bring these things to our attention so as to respond before God and acknowledge our need for a deeper work from Him. Here we open our vessels and ask Him to fill us with His glory that glorifies Him alone.

There are many Christians who offer many kinds of opinions and answers, but until the condition of simple faith that reflects the power of God is met, let them remain silent.

How do we then please God? It is all by faith! So what does Jesus call faith? Is it something I can have? Most certainly it is. And outside of it, we can never please God!

The centurion

I want to look at what Jesus, the perfect man of faith, said about faith. When Jesus heard the words of the centurion, He marveled and called it faith! After I was baptized with the Holy Spirit I saw very clearly the spiritual structure of the heavenly kingdom. I recognized that I am now a man under authority and can never believe or walk on my own ideas.

Let us carefully consider the whole account and we will get understanding.

> And when Jesus was entered into Capernaum, there came unto him a centurion, beseeching him, And saying, Lord, my servant lieth at home sick of the palsy, grievously tormented. And Jesus saith unto him, I will come and heal him. The centurion answered and said, Lord, I am not worthy that thou shouldest come under my roof: but speak the word only, and my servant shall be healed. For I am a man under authority, having soldiers under me: and I say to this man, Go, and he goeth; and to another, Come, and he cometh; and to my servant, Do this, and he doeth it. When Jesus heard it, he marvelled, and said to them that followed, Verily I say unto you, I have not found so great faith, no, not in Israel (Matthew 8:5-10).

The centurion understood the secret to faith and God's working on earth from heaven. Faith is the link that brings heaven's will to earth. This connection is missing in so many who profess Christ. In my understanding, there are few things more important than this truth concerning the life of the believer. I will explain this account of the centurion in greater detail a bit later. So many think they have an understanding of this precept, but they are far from it, as far as the east is from the west.

First, I believe it is of great importance to bring a subject to our attention so that someone might find deliverance from their hardened condition.

There are different characters in Bible history who were defiant against God's kingdom builders. Several of these were Korah and company, Jezebel, the voice of Absalom, and the bulls of Bashan which encompassed King David. The bulls of Bashan are mentioned in the words that foretold of Jesus in Psalm 22:12. The book of Jude also describes actions of the bulls of Bashan, as I understand it.

This defiance in human character is designed to destroy everything in God's kingdom structure. I have met those who try to give input on this subject but are held unaware in a state of blindness. Most who cannot break from this stronghold are plagued with a curse-like stubbornness that offers what I call mysterious blindness as a replacement for God's protocol of order. The mysterious enticement of blindness is a sort of pipe dream and notion of a super-spiritual imagination that is irrational and nonsensical. It is strategically designed against the Holy Spirit's anointing on a leader. These are unrealistic adaptations of spiritual deception in high places.

Men with these forms of stubbornness are creators of systematic mayhem in a structure of spiritual virtue and heavenly order. These are well described in the book of Jude. They bear not enough respect within their sloppy, irreverent hearts to honor God's placement of gifts, callings, and spiritual dignity. Their lofty opinions are highly respected, even though they may destroy a God-given order of unity and love. These are treacherous persons, admiring themselves and appearing super-spiritual.

These seldom-exposed persons are dreamers who are secretly on a pedestal and are not mindful of God's spiritual disposition, standards, and protocol. How must one overcome when such deep dilemma occurs? This is an enormous problem. It can often be detected by a narrative laced in rebellion that causes mistrust and suspicion, especially against spiritual leadership.

The results are that such individuals are beleaguered with torment that is seldom recognized because they are dreamers. In the Bible, these are classified as "filthy dreamers." Dreamers are swingers of the imagination, always learning but never able to come to the knowledge of the truth. They are seldom honest and upright about their own condition, because they are dreamers. A dreamer can be on his face, crying, but the delusion comes, and the finger always points elsewhere. Dreamers never fit in anywhere, and so they are loners and segregate themselves. One of the discerning factors in the life of such a person of danger is that they cannot hear correctly. Their communicative ability is strong in speaking, but they are unable to hear without interference from their dreamy mentality.

Dreamers are hard against God's order, because there is no place for a dreamer in the protocol of God's order. These are unstable enemies of the cross of Christ. These people are never submitted in the succession of any order but stand on their own pinnacle of importance.

The spiritual rebellion of this condition is among the most evil because it is disguised in sheep's clothing. Jeremiah encountered this condition, and we are warned about it in Hebrews as well.

> And they said, There is no hope: but we will walk after our own devices, and we will every one do the imagination of his evil heart (Jeremiah 18:12).

> Take heed, brethren, lest there be in any of you an evil heart of unbelief, in departing from the living God (Hebrews 3:12).

If God's mercy reaches such a person's hardened and disloyal heart, he will fall upon his face before God with no deadlines in mind. This repentance is not a simple one. It is one that resigns every thought, dream, imagination, and design against God's protocol of order. Repentance must accept the monster it has become and rest every case it invented. This poor soul will plead to God for dramatic change: "I need change, or I will die without hope. I will not walk until you change my feet, my eyes, my ears, my heart, my pride, my whole demeanor!"

Few find repentance over this awful condition because the dreaming does not want to quit. A two-minute moment of repentance for a twenty-year problem? Hardly.

There has to be clear recognition of the monster of wrong concepts and conditions of rebellion against God. This repentance needs to correct wrong concepts from satanic persuasions. It has to recognize that its deception is baseless rebellion, designed to destroy God's order of command. Without fail, this deception presents itself as a burden or concern, and the path of destruction plagues descendants into the future. Always take note of this—it never fails. This is the ultimate fallout if there is no repentance of this condition.

One must recognize that the origin of this problem is largely the result of a hearing problem. This problem will not vanish into the distant past by formulas that are implemented with disciplinary strength. Repentance is about a deep, unconditional surrender to what God says. It is a deep surrender to the foundational principles of God's truth. We must come into surrender to what we once perceived as foolishness and walk humbly in the ways of God. Here spiritual, heavenly wisdom begins to be the foundational conduit of the voice of God.

One must be brought beyond humility and walk in a depth of surrender that religion and self-importance never allow. The spiritual application of this truth has to come from a deep and desperate spiritual transformation of the mind and heart. This place of surrender is so unfathomable that most would not go there for fear of loss of reputation and their position of self-importance. Only the most desperate will find this narrow road.

The Jezebel rebellion was the first to counter God's order. The voice of Absalom was the next one to counter God's order. Next was Korah and company, and the worst and final one is the bulls of Bashan rebellion.

I will now try to describe what Jesus saw when He proclaimed that He had witnessed a faith not seen in all of Israel. The following is an interpretation of what the centurion said to Jesus.

When I speak to a certain man in management and ask for something to be completed with specific instructions, if he is under authority, it will be done as requested. If he is in authority it will falter.

Being *under* authority is the key to the successive order of unified effort. If authority is understood as a subordinate function, then all will work like clockwork.

Example: I am the owner of the team, and so the first in the command chain. I make a request, which is turned into a command only if it is received. Now my authority is validated, my subordinate's authority is validated, and his subordinate's authority is validated. All will work like clockwork, and all falls into place and the project will be perfectly finished as authorized. This is extremely important.

If one of these men decides he knows better or mistrusts his authority, he invalidates the authority above him and the order of the first commander becomes invalidated and breached. The fury of the first commander is now at the doorstep of that man and everyone subjected to him. The end result is incomplete and all is chaos.

In this example, I have four under authority. If I, the first commander, choose to bypass the chain of command and go to the third in line to accomplish my request, I will create mistrust and ugly failure in the whole system. I can never do this, because I also am under authority, even though I am the one in the highest rank. Why? I am under the authority of the framework that I have established in the beginning.

This is the protocol of how God's spiritual kingdom works on earth, the same as it is in heaven. If I breach this principle, all is a mess and in disarray, with angry commanders not knowing who to trust or what to do. Satan will try to cause his agents of influence to disrupt the flow, the anointed unity that comes from God, Jesus, and the Holy Spirit, through the command center of God's order known as His kingdom. This spiritual principle of the kingdom is called *faith* from the mouth of Jesus Himself.

Let us go back to the account of Jesus' encounter with the centurion who needed healing for his servant.

> The centurion answered and said, Lord, I am not worthy that thou shouldest come under my roof: but speak the word only, and my servant shall be healed. For I am a man under authority, having soldiers under me: and I say to this man, Go, and he goeth; and to another, Come, and he cometh; and to my servant, Do this, and he doeth it (Matthew 8:8-9)

This commanding officer had one of his ranking servants ill and in torment with an incurable sickness. The centurion said he was not worthy for Jesus to come under his roof to heal the dying servant. Jesus said this man had the greatest faith in all of Israel.

This is exactly how faith works. The centurion made a profound statement. What was it? "I am a man under authority."

This man was under the authority of his own structure. That structure had a roof. He said, "Speak the Word only!" He understood roof, rank, and authority. Then he explained his basis for faith. He declared that if Jesus would only speak the Word, it would be so—because he knew that the mighty works that came from Jesus showed that Jesus was also under authority and had received commands from the Father.

> But that the world may know that I love the Father; and as the Father gave me commandment, even so I do (John 14:31).

Let us go back to a previous example. God created all things by the Word. Jesus is the Word. And God was the Word, and has spoken the Word by the Holy Spirit.

Remember a prior statement? *So God said, Jesus said, the Holy Spirit said, what do I say?* Through this chain of command, God's authority is validated, Jesus' authority is validated, and His subordinates' authority is validated.

I see this mighty power through the spoken Word of God! Here we need to understand the importance of the phrase, "Speak the Word only." According to the centurion, if Jesus would speak the Word only, it would be so. This is exactly how the world was created.

My dear friend, Jesus is the Word, and it is fully spoken. Yes, it is finished! "By His stripes ye were healed" is the Word spoken! Let it be so by faith, because it is so. Let us never take away from or add to the spoken Word of God.

I find that people who do not understand or walk in this principle are not used mightily by God. Their hearts might be ever so kind or eager to do the will of God, but until this principle of authority is within the foundation of a spiritual man, he will avail little for the kingdom of God. If anything, he will make a mess in the work of God.

This man can be impressive in achievements by his own power. But if done without the power of divine dependence upon God and His Word, his work can become a massive tower with huge building blocks of wood, hay, and stubble. When the fire of God starts to purify what seems to be impressive to the eyes of man, there will be a cry of appeal, "Oh, that Ishmael might live before God!"

This is the exact problem that Lucifer had when he left his ranks of authority in heaven and esteemed his opinion better than God's. This is also the precise problem that Eve had when she left her ranks of authority and esteemed her opinion better than God's spoken Word.

Oh, how I cringe when I give someone instructions on the smallest details and while I am speaking they are not hearing. I immediately know that this person does not understand authority, and I can never make him useful with any responsibility. But the mind is set, because the foundation of their heart is biased toward what they want to hear. They lack the principle of authority and run greedily toward the error of Balaam and speak evil of things they have no understanding of.

> But these speak evil of those things which they know not: but what they know naturally [meaning preconceived ideas], as brute beasts, in those things they corrupt themselves. Woe unto them! for they have gone in the way of Cain, and ran greedily after the error of Balaam for reward, and perished in the gainsaying of Core (Jude 10-11).

They corrupt themselves in the things they know naturally. Take great notice in this! These are natural brute beasts, corrupting themselves with things they know by what they hear and see from their natural senses.

> But chiefly them that walk after the flesh in the lust of uncleanness, and despise government. Presumptuous are they, self-willed, they are not afraid to speak evil of dignities (2 Peter 2:10).

They are like Cain, Balaam, Korah, Absalom, Jezebel, and the bulls of Bashan. What else do these do? They have no understanding of dominion in the structure of God's kingdom.

> Likewise also these filthy dreamers defile the flesh, despise dominion, and speak evil of dignities (Jude 8).

I want to give several examples of wrong hearing in natural things.

Someone from a distance had called me for an appointment to speak with me about spiritual struggles he was facing. The specific date was decided, but the time was a bit difficult to determine for both of us, since he lived several hours away and he had committed to a certain project which must be completed first and could affect his time of travel and arrival. He agreed to call me when he started his drive on the specific day.

What I did not tell him was that my wife and I would be gone in the afternoon, because she wanted me to join her at an event that lasted several hours.

The day arrived, and I was anticipating his call. I did not hear from him—the phone was silent. Then it was long past the time I expected him, and I thought perhaps he had given up the appointment.

Later in the afternoon, he called and wondered exactly where I lived and said he would be there in several minutes. I told him I had been waiting for a phone call when he left from his home (as agreed)—and now I was 45 minutes from our place of meeting.

He replied that he had thought it was not necessary to call me when he left home, and he chose not to do so. He arrived at my place long before I did and sat there, seething and ready to vomit all kinds of guilt and anger on me. He certainly did so in a demeaning and disrespectful way when I arrived.

He was very upset, and the meeting ended with me saying almost nothing. He just "let me have it" for more than an hour. Being a servant of God, I said not a word about his neglect in calling me, nor did I tell him I was not at fault. I was as a lamb to the slaughter and opened not my mouth.

After he left our meeting, he left a trail of hate and spite against me—for his own fault. This man has had many problems since, and they are even more than he already had before this incident.

You see, when you are under authority, you need not know more than the instructions and simple obedience to what is authorized. This man left my place and is still angry, and for more than five years he has continued to spread ill will against me. This man had a hearing problem.

A second example: Recently, a person felt it was urgent that he speak to me on a specific day. My schedule was full for that day, but I told him to text me at a certain time for the appointment he was requesting, whenever he had some time. He said he would text me in the forenoon of that day as was planned.

I did not tell him *not* to text me the night before (because I was conducting a meeting at a large function), but I *did* tell him to text me the morning of our planned meeting day. He did not hear correctly, and thought that texting the evening before was no problem.

I answered the next morning as was agreed, and he was not happy and acted obnoxious and upset that I had not responded the evening before.

Why am I making these points?

Because people like this are not people of great faith. They do not hear correctly. They will continue in their folly and wake up one day to see that they are a complete failure in everything, and they won't know why. These people all have a problem with hearing. These are people who hold no understanding of one of the most elementary truths in the entire Bible in surrendering and understanding the structural equilibrium of God's balance of authority.

Here is the list of problems of people who hear what they want to hear. In this rebellion, we find the perfect breeding grounds for discouragement, depression, employment problems, family problems, and problems in every scenario where they are in a position under authority.

These people are individualistic wanderers, filled with many answers for everyone but subdued and saturated with personal defeat. A person who does not understand the structural balance of authority will form a wall of defiance against the true helping hand. The sad fact is that these people often want to be used for the kingdom of God but are seldom used in a spiritual way that leaves a lasting impact on anyone.

When Jesus took notice that the centurion was a man under authority who understood how it all works, He marveled greatly! Should we not also notice and correct our ways, lest we miss who God is able to use?

Find men who are disorganized, and you will find a sluggard who God cannot use for His glory in greater things. These men are tramps who leave sloppy footprints in the finest places. They are irresponsible and foaming waves of trouble, who are never settled nor grounded in rest and security within the peace of God.

> Take heed therefore how ye hear: for whosoever hath, to him shall be given; and whosoever hath not, from him shall be taken even that which he seemeth to have (Luke 8:18).

Faith like a mustard seed

One of the profound statements Jesus made concerning faith is the comparison of faith to a mustard seed. I wanted to correctly define the type of mustard seed that Jesus spoke of, lest there be a question on technicalities.

Pliny the Elder, who lived between AD 23 and AD 79, wrote about the mustard plant in his encyclopedia *Natural History*. He described it as growing "entirely wild, though it is improved by being transplanted: but on the other hand, when it has once been sown, it is scarcely possible to get the place free of it, as the seed when it falls germinates at once." (Pliny, *Natural History*, 19.170-171; Rackham et al. 5.528-529)

There is a difference between the wild mustard plant and one planted in the garden for use in medicines or cooking, yet all types have the same characteristics. In the garden, the mustard plant's growth habits overtake and overpower other plants with which it co-habits. Wild in the field, it quickly spreads and is, as Pliny wrote, almost impossible to get rid of.

I searched multitudes of scholarly opinions and writings, from both ancient and modern day scientists, in a tireless effort to define the exact name and plant that Jesus referred to in His statement about the mustard seed. I researched numerous technical explanations from expositors, authors, scholars, professors, and many well-meaning people on this area of discussion. Studies on the specific mustard plants grown in Israel arrived at several varying conclusions of what type of seed Jesus might have used as an example in His parable.

Several species would have some of the same character traits, and they would also fit well with what Jesus was saying in His statement concerning faith. My honor and respect go to those whose studies are available. However, the results are vastly inconclusive and differ greatly. Many conclusions also do not fit the technical characteristics written about in the Gospels.

After my own extensive research, I have drawn a conclusion, primarily based on the description spoken by Jesus Himself. My conclusion is a simple one: The central image in the parable is that the mustard plant is a dangerous domestic variety or an intrusive kind. This might be a surprise to many—because how could a plant with such characteristics be paralleled to the kingdom of heaven?

Christ spoke of the mustard seed as a large tree deriving from a tiny seed. The plant grows tall and provides protection for birds from predatory hawks as well as from animals. It is a resting place and offers cooling from the extreme heat in the deserts of Israel. The mustard tree that Jesus spoke about is an invasive type of plant. If it is cut to the roots, a new plant starts to grow from the cut area. It is nearly impossible to annihilate.

Now let us look at these verses and then at the application to our personal life.

> And the apostles said unto the Lord, Increase our faith. And the Lord said, If ye had faith as a grain of mustard seed, ye might say unto this sycamine tree, Be thou plucked up by the root, and be thou planted in the sea; and it should obey you (Luke 17:5-6).

Many look at this verse and are overwhelmed, thinking *If my faith is no greater than the tiniest of seeds, I must have no faith,* and they accept defeat and the impossibility of ever pleasing God.

Many think this verse refers to faith "the size" of a small mustard seed. But it does not say "size." When I saw that Jesus said faith "as a grain of mustard seed," I looked into what the grain of mustard seed was like. Why was the tiny seed of this tree used as a true description of faith the way God sees it?

The revelation of truth in this example is among the most powerful illustrations I have ever observed concerning the faith of a child of God. It is a deeply life-changing truth!

What is so profound about this truth of the tiny mustard seed? After this tiny seed has been placed into the ground, it becomes a plant that is virtually impossible to destroy. (I was told by someone from Israel that the only way to destroy it is through many applications of harsh chemical sprays over a period of time.) If this plant is cut down, it springs up in the very places where it was cut. The cut it suffers will be bed to quickly produce new growth.

Deeply-tested spiritual faith works this exact way! The more it is persecuted, the more it grows new strength and develops new sprouts and vigor that flourishes in the kingdom of God.

Beyond the contemporary challenges of the Christian's life, there are those who have advanced under the anointing of the Holy Spirit into depths few would dare to endure. These are the ones who have suffered deeply for His righteousness' sake. They have survived the killing fields of what is popular and highly esteemed among highest religion and cultural traditions. They are a classified few, known only to a few as good soldiers in the fight of faith.

This is why I have spent so much time in previous chapters examining the deeper work of the Spirit: to lay the foundation for this truth.

The deeper virtue of God's work brings such a deep work of faith and purifying of the saint that he becomes an extremely intricate person of true cause. These are the trusted ones of God in His kingdom on earth. The heavenly life stream they know makes them no candidate for obnoxious spiritual repressiveness. The depths of these sanctified ones are protectively isolated within the wisdom of the Holy Spirit. They are the offering before the throne of God. They are the incense burning in the Holy Place. They serve Him in the day and through the night. The tranquility of their souls is not fermented with sensational enticements. They are no more detoured by personal vendettas against God's purpose. Even though they walk among delusional persuasions that seem legitimate, they refuse to bow to seemingly harmless idols because they smell the source. The hearts of these believers will no more be swayed by deceptive accusations against them. Self-proclaimed prophets and gainsayers among religions and cultures hold no light to guide their path. The Holy Spirit is the only one who leads these men of God. They are surrendered to one purpose, and that one purpose is not their own or another man's ideas.

The truth of what Jesus said is heavenly! He draws the parallels between the man of faith and the tiny seed of mustard. This revelation is a colossal illustration of which few Christians have understanding. There are things that Jesus said to His followers that most people either do not understand or else seek to neutralize with reason. Three of these verses are quoted below.

> Verily, verily, I say unto you, He that believeth on me, the works that I do shall he do also; and greater works than these shall he do; because I go unto my Father. And whatsoever ye shall ask in my name, that will I do, that the Father may be glorified in the Son. If ye shall ask any thing in my name, I will do it (John 14:12-14).

The fact that these are the words of Christ does not present us the option or authority to question, to doubt, or to refuse to accept them. This Word is as much the Word of God as any other verse in the Holy Bible. Christ spoke this Word to His disciples and to those whom He would call his own. This is written to the dispensation of the new covenant provision to Israel and the Gentiles. These verses are written to His believers alone.

Mustard seed faith is not personal performance of advanced achievements in any human form. It is the complex triumph by the power of the Holy Spirit within the believer in the face of unfathomable spiritual adversity and anguish. These situations are not unusual encounters to the one who is a truly surrendered cross-bearing saint, and these situations can only be overcome by faith in the promised provision.

Spiritual adversity and anguish do a deep work in the true believer. This refiner's fire achieves an exceeding weight of glory that will only be revealed in the last day.

Many do not understand the depth of these children of God. They are misunderstood by the shallow and maligned by the well-thought-of boasters. These apostles of Christ's righteousness are of vehement detriment to the self-righteous. Men with these attributes are the ones who move the kingdom of God by simple obedience. This is the faith needed, and it rests in the sovereignty of God's true ones.

God uses these fellows to speak to the tall, enormous mountains and strongholds in communities, homes, families, churches, and wherever He leads their feet. These men of God are not the ones who carry a chip on their shoulder and call themselves prophets. These men are not the ones who hold untempered boldness acquired before they knew God. These are men of many tears who carry the mission of God's purpose on earth.

These are men who speak the voice of God among the deprived. The Holy Spirit leads these men in the face of spiritual obstacles that are not overcome by argument, but by faith. Here they speak to the mountains and tell them to go to the same place Jesus sent the Gergesene devils—into the swine and into the sea! They speak to the stubborn sycamine tree, and tell it to be plucked up by the root and drowned in the sea!

Notice that mountains and mulberry trees are used to describe obstacles to faith? A mountain is the enormous silhouette of death that stares destructive impossibilities into a life in a valley. It seeks to buckle your knees and cause you to run in despair, giving up in the valley of decisions.

The mulberry tree is a messy tree that is seldom useful for humans. It feeds the fowl of the air and the fowl find rest in it. It signifies the presence of sour fruit and nesting places of the powers of darkness upon someone. These are conditions of strongholds or unfortunate circumstances and evil encounters. The mulberry is also an invasive plant that is hard to destroy. This is why it has to be pulled by the root or else it will find growth again. Many problems that people and churches face need to be pulled up by the root and cast into the sea!

The mountain and the mulberry are not moved by methodology, but by speaking the word of faith. This is a powerful exercise that can only be done by the ones who have mustard seed faith. God has equipped these agents of His truth to deal with spiritual high places that prevail at times through generations of unholy precepts in captivity.

These of mustard seed faith are the deliverers who come out of Zion, the ones spoken of by the prophet.

> And saviours shall come up on mount Zion to judge the mount of Esau; and the kingdom shall be the LORD's (Obadiah 21).

The spiritually refined people of God will be saviors to the forlorn truth seekers. These fine-linen saints will be saviors of the desolated human thought and reason like the dismay of Eve in Eden. They will show forth the praises of God through radiating once more the ability of Elohim at the close of the age.

There is much courage in this army of men with mustard seed faith. They will bind together with one heart, even crossing denominational lines to protect by example the truth and the righteousness that is by faith.

CHAPTER 7

Works of Faith

Why is faith without works dead?
Are works without faith dead?
Is salvation all faith or all grace?

These questions have been points of heated debate among many people of faith through the ages.

Can we look at the Word of God and draw conclusions, lest we miss the whole point that is being made?

Faith is not an illusion or a dreamy consolation. Faith is a shouldered concern that bears responsibility for the circumstances toward which it is led. Faith does not speak clothing to the naked or declare food to the hungry. It concerns itself with the responsibility of supplying toward the need.

This is the "works" part of faith that all Christians need to have. This is not specifically speaking about a faith food-and-clothing program, as some would promote. It is an example of the fulfillment of the final necessity, whether through faith or works.

> If a brother or sister be naked, and destitute of
> daily food, And one of you say unto them, Depart
> in peace, be ye warmed and filled; notwithstanding
> ye give them not those things which are needful to
> the body; what doth it profit? Even so faith, if it
> hath not works, is dead, being alone (James 2:15-
> 17).

When we see a deceased person, we understand the spirit of
the man has departed. We actually recognize that the person
is not there anymore. So it is, if someone has faith without
works. The active part is not present. This is the way God sees
it: If one is all faith with no works, he is likened as dead.

Faith is not stingy but abundant in giving toward necessity,
whether the giving is in time or material. It carries a spiritual
responsibility to fulfill needs at hand. The Good Samaritan
did not (that we know of) pray for the wounds of the poor
battered man, but supplied the oil and wine because he carried
the means to help with him. When the naked one asks for a
shirt and you have one, give it to him. Sometimes the naked
man is naked because he is lazy. Other times, his condition is
the result of a misfortune. Now pray that God would change
his financial situation, and there can be a wonderful miracle.

The illustrations given in James are practical. I believe faith
is completely practical as well. In other words, if the naked
man is prayed over and clothes do not arrive, for goodness
sake, give him a shirt. In such a case, faith prays believing and
works give. At times, there is only one correct way to approach
this.

The question is debated concerning salvation. Works cannot save us. Our work of spiritual duty can save someone else, but not ourselves. God has not accepted any plan of works by our own performance that will save us. It is His works that save us. His works are the provision for our salvation, and His alone.

However, we have to come to a place of acknowledgment of our sin and need and then turn to Jesus in repentance for forgiveness and trust in His provision to be saved. That is a form of works. Here, works activate our faith; and sometimes, faith activates our works.

But if one is all works with no faith, he is as dead as the one who has all faith and no works.

A universal guilt, fueled by our fallible nature, keeps the carnal man busy with works. There is, perhaps, great intention, but the works could be as deadly as Uzzah's hand that steadied the Ark when it looked as though it was falling (2 Samuel 6:1-7 and 1 Chronicles 13:9-12).

When David heard of Uzzah's death for a single hand put forth to "help," he did not want the Ark to be near him, but sent it to the threshing floor of Nachon. He was grieved that God would do this to a kind-hearted man of his own. "How can we serve a God such as this?" he asked.

The depth of this truth cannot be seen by the casual saint, bedazzled by the world. This truth surrounds those only who seek the deeper effectiveness of God.

How faith and works act together is dependent on the circumstance and the necessity at hand. What is important is that our works as well as our faith can be a spiritual tool.

How can a person become spiritual?

How can a person become spiritual? It is not how often a person thinks about God that makes him spiritual. Nor is it how he concerns himself about religious matters. Becoming a spiritual man is nothing that can be performed by the self man.

> Verily, verily, I say unto you, Except a corn of wheat fall into the ground and die, it abideth alone: but if it die, it bringeth forth much fruit. He that loveth his life shall lose it; and he that hateth his life in this world shall keep it unto life eternal (John 12:24-25).

Herein is the spiritual transformation from being a carnal Christian to being a spiritual Christian. I maintain that if a person comes to a complete spiritual death in all his ways, then by the resurrection by the Holy Spirit he becomes alive. The mighty resurrection power of the Holy Spirit is what makes someone spiritual, but the Holy Spirit cannot resurrect someone who has not died to all they have and are.

Apostle Paul exemplified "I die daily" as the normal for his life. Spiritual death is dying to our own willpower and the thought process of the natural mind. The resurrection is then being in the will of God and having the mind of Christ.

This becomes a spiritual product, whether it is faith or works or a result of combined faith and works. I would declare that after this rendering of a heart and mind, faith and works are unified within by the work of the Holy Spirit.

Abram's dying abilities stood before him as he frustrated the strength of his own way. He was getting to be a very old man, and when he finally recognized that it was no more possible to father a child by trying, he exhausted the natural avenue, trying to enter into the promise by his own process. He saw the promise but could not enter into the faith required to cause the miracle of God to produce his offspring.

As far as works, he had done it all correctly—to no avail. Abram was now 99 years old. He had tried so hard to be the perfect man that God could bless in fulfilling the promised lineage of millions in future generations—namely, the generation of faith. After all this, God met him and asked him to be perfect!

> And when Abram was ninety years old and nine, the Lord appeared to Abram, and said unto him, I am the Almighty God; walk before me, and be thou perfect. And I will make my covenant between me and thee, and will multiply thee exceedingly (Genesis 17:1-2).

Abram had only one place to go after God asked him for perfection that would bring forth the promise he tried to fulfill for many years. Verse 3 says "And Abram fell on his face." When he rose back up, God said he was to be called Abraham.

What had happened? Abram went down one man and came up another man. Same person, but different man! The

H was put into his name. God also commanded that Sarai would now be "Sarah," also adding an *H*.

If you pronounce the letter *H* in almost all languages, it produces a current of air. The Holy Spirit is described in Hebrew and Greek as "a current of air." That current of air is what causes one to receive the promises of God in all phases of life. That current of air will change one from carnal thinking to spiritual thinking. Change good ideas to spiritual guidance. Change personal abilities to God's capability.

Now the impossible becomes possible. And Isaac became the spiritual product because God did the miracle. Years later, God asked that the miracle be placed upon the altar, and the works of Abraham became spiritual. Previously, his works were carnal, and he could not produce anything except Ishmaels.

Many remain unchanged and untouched by the Holy Spirit's inner working because they lack desire for spiritual usefulness. We are content with ineffectiveness. The divine work of the potter does not happen if we do not welcome the embrace of the Holy Spirit in the form He chooses.

The spiritual man is brought into places that look absolutely insurmountable to him. He often stands in question in the deepest sense. He is brought into a valley of dejection over the burden of the calling upon him. His future is in question, and his direction is dissolved. He becomes a glaring beacon of misinterpretation. This is a place where heaven seems silent. This is where Satan's transforming agents of light spring up, filled with diverting answers. The only things to guide him are the shadows of the Urim and Thummin upon his mantle, the past battle armor of his victories, and the tear-filled nights of his Gethsemanes.

God sees this picture as a transition to a deeper walk and function in the kingdom of God. Out of these threshing floors come resurrection, and at times redirection.

The carnal Christian has no knowledge of these brooks of Cherith. This was the brook where Elijah was sent by God, and then the brook dried up. There are many who go through sorrows that they create themselves, but it is because of their own sin. These are always learning but do not come to the knowledge of the truth by experience.

> And I, brethren, could not speak unto you as unto spiritual, but as unto carnal, even as unto babes in Christ. I have fed you with milk, and not with meat: for hitherto ye were not able to bear it, neither yet now are ye able (1 Corinthians 3:1-2).

Can brethren in Christ be classed as carnal? Most definitely so!

A carnal man finds offense in a spiritual man because he does not walk or understand in the same way. A spiritual man's finest intentions arising from a pure heart are never really understood by the carnal Christian. Since the carnal man cannot receive from the Spirit of God, he also stands in opposition to the spiritual man.

The depth of the purpose of the spiritually resurrected man goes much deeper than the natural eye can comprehend. The realm where the spiritual man operates is extremely controversial to the natural man, because the natural man cannot receive the things of the Holy Spirit. The spiritual man does receive things from the Holy Spirit. Here we see the difference of vision, light, and revelation.

The natural man cannot see into this heavenly place, nor can he enter into it. The position of usefulness in Christ is far above all principalities and powers. This is a fellowship of God's divine holiness, and it's a mystery to the carnal mind.

> And to make all men see what is the fellowship of the mystery, which from the beginning of the world hath been hid in God, who created all things by Jesus Christ: To the intent that now unto the principalities and powers in heavenly places might be known by the church the manifold wisdom of God (Ephesians 3:9-10).

The cloud that stood between the children of Israel and Pharaoh and his army near the Red Sea gave light to Israel, but it blinded the Egyptian soldiers. The blindness in the Egyptian elite took no notice of Israel's guiding cloud. The Egyptian military depended on their strategic maneuvers to push Israel into the channel of Nuweiba by the Red Sea. The army of Pharaoh was seeing an immense victory as they looked at the impossible crossing at the sea. What Egypt did not see is that it was the cloud that led Israel, not the army that pushed them.

They who are led by the Spirit of God, they are the sons of God. A large majority of professing Christians know very little about being led by the Spirit of God, but this is the pivotal point of transition from man's works to spiritual production through a man by the living Spirit of God.

If a man is a spiritual man, can works then be a spiritual tool? If it comes from a spiritual person who has been transformed and walks by faith, then even his works can be a spiritual act.

When the Holy Spirit is the source of power, His empowerment fulfills the need, whether it is through works or faith. The work of that person is now a spiritual work and is maintained through daily dying to self and resurrection empowered by the Holy Spirit.

> If one is all works with no faith, he is as dead as the one who has all faith and no works.

Does faith produce works or do works produce faith? Which one did Abraham have when he walked up the rugged path onto Mount Moriah to place his son Isaac upon the altar? Here he was justified by the works of personal surrender of the gift of promise he had received.

> Was not Abraham our father justified by works, when he had offered Isaac his son upon the altar? Seest thou how faith wrought with his works, and by works was faith made perfect? (James 2:21-22).

Here were works that made faith perfect. It was by his falling upon his face and then rising up in spiritual faith that caused Abraham and Sarah to conceive Isaac. However, Abraham also had to do the work of natural reproduction to produce conception. In other words, there was no child without a sexual relationship.

His acknowledgment of his personal inability to reproduce with Sarai was the key here. Abram was well able to reproduce with Hagar, an act which was not promise-based. Abram could not produce the promise that was given him by God concerning Sarai. The son he could not produce was the promised son who would begin the lineage of generations like the stars in the heaven and sand by the shore.

We must grip this truth, lest we miss the spiritual usefulness that God wants us to fulfill on the earth. This effectiveness is the difference between building with wood, hay, and stubble compared to building with gold, silver and precious stone, which is much less visible to the natural eye.

God is the master architect, and it is His call that develops one's spiritual thinking. Many do not understand that the promises of God are nothing achievable by human performance alone. The rod of Moses must be placed upon the impassable Red Sea before the waters open up and become God's intended passage. This is how faith and works are partners of duty to make faith perfect.

> Ye see then how that by works a man is justified, and not by faith only (James 2:24).

Jesus did a deed of faith every time he healed someone, whether it was in speaking, touching, lifting by the hand, laying on of the hand, making a paste of mud, or breaking the crust of the bread.

Once the crust of retention around the bread was broken, the power of His touch released the growth of the bread, and like resurrection life, it exploded in a way the world had never seen. The abundance of bread must have burst out, like a swelling under pressure that would not stop till thousands were filled. Hallelujah!

Likewise, the spear thrust into the side of Jesus opened the stream of blood that brought forgiveness and released water that cleansed the world. The blood and water came after Jesus' final human breath. Until the old wineskins are broken, there is no necessity of new wineskins. The works of our labor must cease and we come to a place of rest where God is the power and the performer of what He desires. Only then will God's manifest wisdom be displayed in the way He desires and He will be glorified.

> There remaineth therefore a rest to the people of God. For he that is entered into his rest, he also hath ceased from his own works, as God did from his. Let us labour therefore to enter into that rest, lest any man fall after the same example of unbelief (Hebrews 4:9-11).

The rest referred to is not a rest someday in heaven. It is rest in the power of the Holy Spirit, as we cease from our own strength and performance.

> For we which have believed do enter into rest, as he said, As I have sworn in my wrath, they shall not enter into my rest: although the works were finished from the foundation of the world (Hebrews 4:3).

The ugly problem here is that it is difficult for the old wineskins to admit defeat. The Cains of the land do their best intention. But that is not what pleases God, and His wrath is upon them.

What pleases God is to see the power of His own Spirit work through the faith of mortal man, in ways not possible by the man of flesh. Herein is God glorified! We are only a vessel. He is our strength and ability.

To those who seek for Him, God presents a better way. He weakens and diminishes our ability and strength through extremely difficult circumstances of powerlessness. The Holy Spirit leads us to dreadful places to turn our strength into weakness. It is in this place only that we solemnly acknowledge "When I am weak, then He is strong."

Weak is rest! And it is God's love that leads us here.

What is this spiritual weakness and how does it disclose itself?

It is an acknowledgment of our inability in the face of a mountain, a task, or a giant, and it is to put us on our face before God.

We can be brought to this place in many ways. It may come through assignments and tasks far too big to accomplish. Sometimes it comes as a problem of health, a problem that makes even the work of God seem impossible.

It is often an excessive, unexpected flood of falsehood against a pure heart. Character annihilation, coming against our obedience and surrendered will to God, can bring deep disappointments. It can be an expression of aggression far too big to handle. It is soul melting and heart wrenching. These things are not the common trades of ordinary trials and tribulations common to man. These are Sauls in David's life and giants to conquer. The giants typically rise in unanticipated ways to destroy God's elect and the anointed ones who bear the heart of God.

The stratagem does not come from the obvious enemy—that would not be a difficult trial to endure and would leave us for the most part unchanged. The attack comes instead from a friend, the trusted one, the carnal Christian, the partner, the close kin. The one we helped and the one we trusted. It often comes through anxiety-driven imaginations of wicked opinions. It comes from betrayers like Judas. It is the spit in the face of Jesus. It is a test and judgment like a trial for death before a tribunal.

This contraction of weakness gets classified as failure and becomes a laughingstock to those of ill-will. It is all intended to make a strong man weak and dissuaded of any strength. It is designed to exceedingly humiliate the saint of God, to instill a sense of worthlessness. It is the trepidation of being misunderstood because of Christ's righteousness within. It is the demolition of the self empire's dream in the face of the scorners.

Abram had to come to this, on his face before the mercy of God, chastened by a love that millions are strangers to.

But all these impossibilities are wonderful fields of harvest. They cause our ability to fail and His to avail. These enormous obstacles become insignificant once the power of God whelms the weakened soul and fills him with the pleasure of God's utmost strength.

This weakness filled with God's power was the angelic bread of Elijah while he ran on for forty days. By it he was thrust onto a path of the unknown future filled with pursuits in the will of God. It created a thirst so deep that he ran hundreds of miles in search of the voice of God at Horeb. Hallelujah!

In the same way, the supernal victory is ours. This spiritual phenomenon is the washing of the robes in the blood of the Lamb. These saints have come through great tribulation and have been made white as snow. They have purged themselves from the accuser of the brethren.

These are saints who serve before the throne of God in the land of the sun and stars, in the day and in the night. These are not in heaven, because in heaven there is no night. These are the saints with God's presence among them. These saints are where God is and where His truth comes forth in clarity. There is no rebellion against the order of His kingdom here.

Oh yes, these are the ones with many tears, but God will wipe away the tears as well. They are well fed as they sail into the eternities of His heavenly presence!

> These are they which came out of great tribulation, and have washed their robes, and made them white in the blood of the Lamb. Therefore are they before the throne of God, and serve him day and night in his temple: and he that sitteth on the throne shall dwell among them. They shall hunger no more, neither thirst any more; neither shall the sun light on them, nor any heat. For the Lamb which is in the midst of the throne shall feed them, and shall lead them unto living fountains of waters: and God shall wipe away all tears from their eyes (Revelation 7:14-17).

The enlightenment of the saints

The rest of this chapter is a call to live in the light of truth revealed by the Holy Spirit. The absence of this light of truth in Christians' lives is one of the great problems of our day.

Over the last forty years' time, in the well-cultured community where I live, I have discovered a gloomy stronghold that has prevailed in keeping many people from going deeper with Christ. I marvel at the glaring shallowness among so many believers. Many have barely any understanding of the promises and truth in God's Word.

Years ago, I prayed to God and said, "If there is no more to the Christian life than what I have experienced to this point, I will never make it. I will be so ineffective that most people will stumble over me like the Pharisaic grave that Jesus describes."

Jesus heard my cry, and in a moment I was overcome by a dramatic, deep spiritual transformation. It was exactly like what happened in the upper room at Pentecost. I was baptized with the Holy Ghost and power.

But I find among many a general fear of the Holy Spirit. People are afraid of the Teacher.

This fear is a tool of Satan to keep truth from being sought out. The delusion of natural reasoning has kept many lives in a darkness that obscures any desire for the deeper things of God. Predetermined ideas against revelations of truth by the Holy Spirit hide the truth written in the Bible, and lives lived in fear of the Holy Spirit show such an infinitesimal trace of His work that there is little evidence that there *is* a Holy Spirit.

We have to die to this problem of fear.

I wish to unveil this subject of living in the light so a deeper desire is produced within the hearts of those who are hungry for more than they presently have.

I believe light is a major component of faith. Light is the first thing that appeared when the wonderful Creator spoke to the earth. He found the earth void and empty, without light. Darkness held its enormous strength over the barrenness.

The word used here in Genesis for darkness is the Hebrew word *choshek*. Its meaning is as follows: darkness, misery, destruction, death, ignorance, sorrow, wickedness (SC 2822). This was the existing condition that the earth was found to be in before God spoke light to it.

What disappeared when darkness disappeared? The power of misery, destruction, death, ignorance, sorrow, and wickedness was lifted and was overtaken by the spoken light. Light was not an imagination but was a word spoken, and the immense power of the word was a visible phenomenon that dispersed darkness and all its effects.

> And the earth was without form, and void; and darkness was upon the face of the deep. And the Spirit of God moved upon the face of the waters (Genesis 1:2).

Numerous things might appear as light but are far from the light of the Holy Spirit and the spoken Word.

Satan is a transformed angel of light. The Bible literally says just that. It does not say that he does this once in a while. It is a clear description of him!

Satanic brightness is never reliable, and it will always do great harm. This form of light will appear to the imagination and cause deviations from real truth. It will do the exact opposite of what light does. It will bring blindness that produces immediate chaos and devastating ruin. It always works as superior and greater in significance than what it tries to conquer. Satanic brightness causes restless and unstable spectators to be swept off their feet, because they are not people who understand God's order. Attention is always drawn toward the one flaunting this brightness, so he gains voice, prominence, and attention. This is the description of the fall of Lucifer.

We read the description of Satan's false light as angelic:

> For such are false apostles, deceitful workers, transforming themselves into the apostles of Christ. And no marvel; for Satan himself is transformed into an angel of light (2 Corinthians 11:13-14).

Who are these false apostles, and what are they doing that Paul is so concerned about? Paul calls them workers. They are workers of deceit, transformed into those claiming apostolic calling. The devastation caused by these false apostles is the evil that will cause well-meaning Christians to run from deeper truth.

The exact meaning of their performance is this: They work deceit by manipulation and imaginary fabrication, trying to undo the work of the Holy Spirit. These workers make something small into something huge, and something huge into something small.

How does Paul deal with these workers? First, he says he will keep on doing what he was doing and will not stop. So we see that false apostles, by buckling your knees in shock, want to cause you to stop what you are doing. But Paul says one must continue to do what God had led true apostles to do. This counteracts what the false apostles are trying to work.

> And I will keep on doing what I am doing in order to cut the ground from under those who want an opportunity to be considered equal with us in the things they boast about (2 Corinthians 11:12 NIV).

By continuing to do what you were led to do by the Holy Spirit, you'll cut the low growth that has been planted and designed to eventually destroy the whole crop in the field. If you quit, the whole field will be overtaken and destroyed.

These workers of iniquity also seek to stimulate the imaginations of a poor soul and cause Eve to fall into disobedient rebellion. When we look at the subject of true light, we have to speak about imagination. It is the most vulnerable tool that humans have, and thus the workers of deceit make it a target.

Those who are held captive by Satan in this framework are held by the vicious disposition of anxiety. These are victims to their minds and are prisoners of imaginations that are atrocious and filled with vain lies. These prisoners will cause great harm to those whom their imaginations have an aversion to. In this picture, you will always find a worker of deceit.

This problem has to be overcome by humble admission, deep penitence, and clear restitution to the victims they have chosen to mistrust. There is no other way to overcome than through deep humility and returning to the true light of Christ.

> Casting down imaginations, and every high thing that exalteth itself against the knowledge of God, and bringing into captivity every thought to the obedience of Christ (2 Corinthians 10:5).

These imaginations we are to cast down are truly one of the biggest instruments that Satan uses against a professing Christian. How?

Darkness cannot overcome light, nor does it ever drive out light. Darkness occupies every square inch of a room where light is not present. We should never fear darkness. Darkness does not clash with light; it is powerless in the presence of light. But we do need to fear when light is reduced and waning. A dimming light allows some darkness. The less light, the more darkness. Diminished light is caused by contamination or a weakened source of power.

This condition exists among souls who profess Christ and are yet held by the strongholds and lusts of sin. If we walk in sin and yet declare that we walk in light, we are deceived. We cannot walk in the light or be guided by the light when darkness is present.

In this condition of faint and feeble light, we mix our natural senses with thoughts and call it "revelation"—and it is only imagination. It is not from God but from our own inclinations, pre-existing conditions in the heart.

Satan falsely illuminated the mind of Eve by a simple question: "Yea, hath God said?" Eve's mind was then caused to question the spoken word of God. The venom shot into her mind, and it became darkened. She imagined in all three aspects of her human functions—the soul, the mind, and the spirit.

Lucifer's question made the tree look good to Eve. Because something happened in the mind of Eve, that which looked so bad and evil when God spoke now took on the appearance of a pleasant tree. The fall of Eve was based in the imagination. Let's look at Eve's confession.

1. Eve now saw that the tree was good for food! *She imagined it.*

2. Eve now saw the evil tree was pleasant to the eyes! *She imagined it.*

3. Eve now saw that this evil tree was a tree desired to make her a wise women! *She imagined it.*

That tree proved to be exactly what God had said and the exact opposite of what Eve imagined.

The fall of humanity in Eden was a betrayal by a deceitful worker who had fallen out of heaven and enticed a perfect human being who knew no sin to imagine against God's order—and all hell broke loose. Millions and millions of people are in hell today because of the deceit of that incident. There cannot be a larger historic earthly catastrophe than what happened that moment amidst the serenity of Eden.

How can someone be so easily deceived? The imagination is appallingly vulnerable to Satan and all his workers, who want to inflame it with falsehood and opinion. A true saint of God has learned to keep this tool from being infested by exterior impressions.

Light and truth

Lest we miss God's desire and total provision for our lives, we need to understand the different sources of light.

God is light, and in Him is no shadow. The light that was spoken over the void and empty earth is what brought order and life to it. The same source of light spoke to Adam and Eve and told them not to eat of the tree that was called knowledge.

But Eve was enticed with natural light—or, that which made sense according to what she saw. She turned to natural understanding for truth when she saw from her soul, spirit, and body, which are the gates to natural human understanding.

She was deceived by natural perception, induced by suggestion to make imagination the source of truth. The natural man cannot receive the things of the Spirit of God;

they are foolishness to him. So she was completely deceived. Natural light will bring our senses into a place of judgment.

What I find is that so many people read the Bible in this way—by depending on natural light, natural reasoning. The result is lukewarmness.

Paul prayed without ceasing concerning the need of the church in Ephesus. That need was for them to receive God's Word through spiritual enlightenment, not natural perception.

> That the God of our Lord Jesus Christ, the Father of glory, may give unto you the spirit of wisdom and revelation in the knowledge of him: The eyes of your understanding being enlightened; that ye may know what is the hope of his calling, and what the riches of the glory of his inheritance in the saints, And what is the exceeding greatness of his power to us-ward who believe, according to the working of his mighty power (Ephesians 1:17-19).

In Paul's prayer concern, he describes the avenue to receive truth. He prayed that the spirit of wisdom, through the revelation of the knowledge of Jesus, might give understanding into the deeper things of the Spirit of God.

When we receive Christ as our Savior and surrender all to Him, He becomes our life source and salvation. This is simply the beginning. Then, at this point, many discontinue and never go any deeper into the Christian life and even lose what was gained.

It is often the condemnation of hidden sin that causes people to stumble and not pursue God.

> And this is the condemnation, that light is come into the world, and men loved darkness rather than light, because their deeds were evil. For every one that doeth evil hateth the light, neither cometh to the light, lest his deeds should be reproved (John 3:19-20).

Their first love becomes a stranger that strangles them with hopelessness, because they see no further than what their natural mind comprehends, and the natural mind cannot receive things from the Spirit of God.

So all comes to a halt, or they turn to all works and motions.

What else do we need? We need to pray for the Holy Spirit to open our hearts to enable us to depart from natural perception and to receive a change of mind so that we can receive spiritual understanding and enlightenment from heaven.

In the tabernacle of Moses, we notice that there are three different degrees of light, typifying degrees of light and truth in our spiritual walk.

1. The natural sunlight in the outer court.

2. The seven golden candlesticks in the Holy Place.

3. The Shekinah glory in the Holy of Holiest.

In the outer court: The entrance into the Tabernacle was in the outer court, where the altar stood to burn the sin offering twenty-four hours a day. This is the place of repentance. Here is the place to confess and forsake our sins. We become distinctly aware of the difference between sins and sin, and we acknowledge that sins are the result of sin. Sin is the root, and sins are the fruit.

The whole chapter of Romans 6 was written to lead us into deliverance from sin, and the honesty around the altar is where our sin is completely dealt with.

This is also the place where we present our body a living sacrifice and are crucified with Christ, "that the body of sin might be destroyed, that henceforth we do not serve sin (Romans 6:6)." Sin shall not have dominion over us anymore.

Entering into this place, we no longer belong to ourselves. We accept the purchased exchange that Jesus made as a ransom for our sins. We are not guilty anymore. We are now forgiven and the price has been paid by the blood of Jesus.

In the Holy Place: The Holy Place, or inner court, is where the consecration offering was presented. This calls for a much deeper and extensive work than simple surrender. It calls for a loss of identity. Aaron was stripped of his tribal garments and dressed in a high priestly robe, now representing heaven and not any one of the tribes of Israel. Many have never consecrated their lives to this depth—the cost is too great. Many cannot lay down their reputation or things of much lesser value. This is where they stop and will not go any deeper into the kingdom of God's purposes.

In the Holy Place is where the ultimate price is paid in complete surrender to God. Here, we do not claim any rights anymore, but learn to walk by faith in the promises provided for our going.

> So likewise, whosoever he be of you that forsaketh not all that he hath, he cannot be my disciple (Luke 14:33).

This is the place where the oil of the crushed olive provides the light coming from seven golden candlesticks. After this process, the Holy Spirit combines with the lamps to illuminate the place.

The Holy of Holies: In the Holy of Holies, the presence of God dwelt upon the Ark of the Covenant. It was the place where the light was the Shekinah glory of God Himself. The strength of this was so great that it was not visible to the human eye.

The outer court was made with brass and wood. The Holy Place was made with refined, beaten gold. The Holy of Holies was made with pure gold! We see that the deeper we are led into the presence of Almighty God, the purer everything becomes.

It is only in faith that we walk here in the Holy of Holies with spiritual boldness. Access to this place was opened when the veil in the temple was rent in two from top to bottom at the moment of Christ's death.

I have done extensive studies for many years on this subject, and this brief summary is not even close to scratching the surface of all that the Tabernacle typified of our spiritual walk.

Ezekiel saw a vision by the revelation of God concerning the problem that existed in Israel's worship.

> And he brought me into the inner court of the LORD's house, and, behold, at the door of the temple of the LORD, between the porch and the altar, were about **five and twenty men**, with their **backs toward the temple of the LORD**, and their **faces toward the east**; and they worshipped the sun toward the east (Ezekiel 8:16).

They were worshipping natural sunlight with their backs turned against the Shekinah glory of God. This is much the sad picture of the powerless church of our day. We have huge numbers, but no power. Strict rules, but no power. There are few who have any depth of understanding in the Word.

Is our worship being instructed by the natural light that comes from the sun of the outer court? Are "good ideas" running the church, or is it by a great business plan that impresses all but God? Are we yet offended by the Shekinah glory of God?

What light is guiding us? Is it the natural light or the Shekinah of God's presence?

Shallow repentance without penitence has filled too many churches. We need the church to begin to weep between the porch and the altar.

Let it begin with us today!

Acknowledgments

I thank my family and many believers who have stood with me for nearly 40 years in solid, unwavering support of the work God has called me to. I thank each one of you.

I give thanks to my editor, Elaine Starner, who has again done an excellent job of taking my message and making it clear to understand and easy to read. The complexities of my writings at times make it difficult to understand, however you do such a tremendous job to makes things clear.

Arlen Miller has spent many hours in preparing this book for print and is ever so willing and eager to promote my work in print. I thank you so kindly, and may God reward you for your tireless effort. You have been sent so the works that God has worked through my life can be recorded for a hungry generation.

Thank you so much to all our early reviewers who have helped improve the presentation of the message of this book.

May this work go forth to the hungry and thirsty of God's children. I bless you for your hearts of sincere love for Jesus and for the whole church family. I stand in awe of how the Lord has rescued so many of our lives from despair, wreckage, and powerlessness and made us children of His mighty Kingdom.